Research Projects and Research Proposals

This book is a guide to writing scientific research proposals for submission to funding agencies. It approaches the topic by placing it in the larger context of planning and carrying out a research project, offering guidance on selecting a suitable research topic, organizing and planning the project, identifying a funding agency, writing the proposal, and managing the funded project. The book also discusses the ethical responsibilities of the researcher, the proposal review process, and how to deal with declination of a proposal.

The author's twenty-five years of experience as an NSF program officer lend the book a unique insider's perspective on the proposal writing and research funding process. Because of that experience, the author is able to anticipate and answer the questions that researchers most frequently ask when preparing to write a proposal, and also to explain how program officers think about proposals when they are making funding decisions.

Paul G. Chapin was director of the National Science Foundation Linguistics Program. He is a member of the Linguistic Society of America and of the American Association for the Advancement of Science.

Research Projects and Research Proposals

A Guide for Scientists Seeking Funding

PAUL G. CHAPIN

With a Foreword by Alan I. Leshner

CAMBRIDGE
UNIVERSITY PRESS

PUBLISHED BY THE PRESS SYNDICATE OF THE UNIVERSITY OF CAMBRIDGE
The Pitt Building, Trumpington Street, Cambridge, United Kingdom

CAMBRIDGE UNIVERSITY PRESS
The Edinburgh Building, Cambridge CB2 2RU, UK
40 West 20th Street, New York, NY 10011-4211, USA
477 Williamstown Road, Port Melbourne, VIC 3207, Australia
Ruiz de Alarcón 13, 28014 Madrid, Spain
Dock House, The Waterfront, Cape Town 8001, South Africa

http://www.cambridge.org

First published 2004

Printed in the United States of America

Typeface Palatino 10/13.5 pt.   *System* LATEX 2$_\varepsilon$ [TB]

A catalog record for this book is available from the British Library.

Library of Congress Cataloging in Publication Data
Chapin, Paul G., 1938–
    Research projects and research proposals : a guide for scientists seeking
funding / by Paul G. Chapin.
        p.   cm.
    Includes bibliographical references and index.
    ISBN 0-521-83015-X – ISBN 0-521-53716-9 (pb.)
    1. Science – Research grants – Handbooks, manuals, etc.   I. Title.
Q180.55.G7C44   2004
507′.973 – dc22   2003069568

ISBN 0 521 83015 x hardback
ISBN 0 521 53716 9 paperback

This book is dedicated to Dr. Richard T. Louttit, Division Director for Behavioral and Neural Sciences at the National Science Foundation from 1975 to 1991.

He has always understood what is important.

Contents

Foreword

Leading a productive research program involves much more than simply running a bunch of experiments. It requires an overarching conceptual framework, a strategic plan for the sequence of studies to be run and, of course, financial support for your work. None of these aspects of a research program are simple, and knowing how to do them is certainly not an innate skill. Unfortunately, many mentors focus their teaching efforts only on the experimental details of doing science. They fall short on teaching their scientific offspring how to conceptualize and lead a full-blown research program. Paul Chapin's expert guide to the planning, support, and conduct of research does a splendid job of laying out both the broad and the nitty-gritty issues of running a research program.

One of the core issues, of course, is funding for your research program. Securing support has become a constant, often nagging facet of modern scientific life. It starts early and never seems to let up. You likely have to worry about how to pay for your graduate education, and you certainly need to think about how you can support your postdoctoral training. Often, you need to write detailed proposals outlining what you would do if you were accepted into the various laboratories to which you have applied. It gets more complex once you are leading your own lab, since you may well need multiple grants to sustain the efforts of a modern, typically complex scientific enterprise. The pervasiveness and persistence of these issues make

Paul Chapin's uniquely insightful and comprehensive guide a must read for every developing scientist.

Dr. Chapin brings the perspective of a long time Federal (NSF) program director who clearly understands all three core perspectives in the proposal funding process – the principal investigator's, the grant reviewer's, and the funding agency official's. It's well worth reading those sections carefully, since to be successful, one needs to understand and respond to these different points of view. And he takes the time in this work to cover all the steps – from planning the project you are about to propose, to actually administering the grant once you get it. This is as close to a cookbook for successfully running a lab as I have ever seen. Chapin also has a nice way of empathizing with the developing scientist, understanding and providing good advice about dealing with some of the emotional, as well as the practical aspects of scientific life.

As one reads through the book, one finds many tips that may seem obvious once said, but might not be followed if left unsaid. One of my favorite quotes from Phillip Abelson, the long-time Editor-in-Chief of the journal *Science* and a codiscoverer of the element Neptunium, is "Where's the Whammy?" It is sometimes difficult to remember that the grant reviewer may not immediately see how very exciting and important your research project idea is, so you need to get his or her attention right up front and then sustain it throughout. Boring is bad. You need to send your major message in the first paragraphs.

Relatedly, Chapin emphasizes the need to be constantly aware of the audience for your proposal. There is an old saying: "Know before whom you stand!" Successful public speakers understand that they need to talk to the audience about what the audience is interested in hearing – and then you can talk about your own special interests along the way. In writing grant proposals, what is so obviously interesting and exciting to you may not be immediately interesting and exciting to someone from even a closely related field. Show them how exciting your project is to your subfield, but also make sure you emphasize right up front why this work is so important from a broader perspective. And leave nothing to the interpretation of the reviewer. What may by now be intuitively obvious to you likely will not be so obvious to the reader. It's your job, not the reader's, to make sure your essential points are well understood.

Read carefully through the sections in this book on the grant review and grant administration processes. Peer review is the most important factor in whether you get your grant or not. It is not a perfect system, since it tends to be somewhat conservative and receives criticism for being somewhat unwilling to support riskier projects, particularly in tight money times. However, everyone in the scientific community agrees it is the best of alternative approaches to deciding who gets funded, and virtually every science supporting agency depends heavily on peer review. As Chapin points out, though, the details of the peer review process differ among agencies, and it is important that you prepare your proposals keeping in mind how they will be reviewed.

Speaking of peer review, it is important to remember that those criticisms you get are not nearly as personal as they feel. Although it is true that some peer reviewers can excessively nit-pick – almost beyond belief – in their attempts to discriminate among proposals – which ultimately is their task – my experience is that most reviewers genuinely want to be helpful. Moreover, in my experience, very few reviews are totally off base, and if the reviewers "just don't understand your work," the fault likely lies much more with your description than with their ignorance. No one likes criticism, and everyone is human. My advice to principal investigators is to read the reviews and then put them aside for a few days before going back and trying to decide which criticisms are valid. And remember: everyone gets proposals declined. Success rates in most agencies hover around the 25–30 percent level. They are higher for established investigators, which means that most younger investigators really do get rejected on the first or second submission. I always think a lifetime success rate of 50 percent is a wonderful accomplishment.

Chapin's lessons in grant administration are equally important. Taking someone else's money bestows responsibilities. Different public and private agencies have different rules and different reporting requirements. If you violate them, the funder will remember!

I found Dr. Chapin's descriptions of the interests and activities of various federal agencies particularly helpful. I would remind the reader that in many fields, there also are many private foundations – some large, some small – who might be interested in supporting your work, particularly in its early stages. Most universities have development offices that can help match you with appropriate private foundations.

Science is a wonderful and rewarding way of life. We live in an era where science and technology are ever more embedded in every societal issue. This makes scientists important contributors to societal progress. Chapin's book helps ease the way into operating smoothly and effectively as a part of the scientific community. My advice is to learn its lessons well.

Alan I. Leshner
Chief Executive Officer
American Association for the Advancement
    of Science

Executive Publisher
Science

After ten years as Professor of Psychology at Bucknell University, Dr. Leshner spent nine years at the National Science Foundation, where he oversaw an array of programs in the biological, behavioral, and social sciences and in science education. He then became the Deputy Director of the National Institute of Mental Health, and from 1994–2001 was the Director of the National Institute on Drug Abuse at the National Institutes of Health.

Acknowledgments

Many people have helped me greatly in writing this book. Let me thank first my most assiduous and persevering readers of the first draft, who kept their comments coming chapter after chapter, providing me both much encouragement and much improvement in the text: Howard Kurtzman, John Yellen, Lloyd Douglas, Penny Firth, Sarah Partan, and Susan Chapin.

Others also provided valuable comments on different parts of the manuscript: Bernard McDonald, Beth Strausser, Catherine Ball, Cecile McKee, Cheryl Eavey, Dan Newlon, Gary Strong, Helen Gigley, John Chapin, Joseph Psotka, Robert Sorkin, Steven Breckler, Stuart Plattner, Susan Chipman, Tracy Gorman, and William Bainbridge. My warm thanks to all.

The book had its origin in a course called "Professionalism in Linguistics" that I taught at the Linguistic Society of America 2001 Summer Institute at the University of California, Santa Barbara. My thanks to Charles Li, the Director of the Institute, for inviting me to participate, and to the students and affiliates who attended the class and gave me great insights on how best to organize and present the material. I especially want to thank two of the class participants, Ellen Barton and Anetta Kopecka, who went above and beyond the call of duty by giving me their reflections on the course after it ended.

Phil Laughlin of Cambridge University Press gave me the encouragement I needed to turn my stack of notes and jumble of thoughts into a book, for which I am very grateful.

Last, and first, and always, my love and gratitude go to my wife, my life's partner, and my best friend, Susan.

Introduction

A scientist's life is exciting but demanding. You have chosen a profession that gives you the opportunity to discover things that no one has ever known, but expects you to devote immense effort to the pursuit of that knowledge. Besides your work in the lab and the library, you are expected to publish the results of your work regularly, to help train the next generation of scientists, and to obtain some of the resources that enable you to do your work.

The aim of this book is to help you with the latter task, by introducing you to the world of research funding.

A great deal of money is available to support scientific research in the United States, and a cultural system has evolved to manage its distribution. The system is no more complex than other cultural systems in our society, but it does have its own norms, traditions, and procedures, which those who wish to participate in it must learn. Scientists need to become familiar with the research funding culture to enjoy the fullest opportunity to achieve their goals. This volume is a guidebook to that culture.

If you are just beginning your scientific career as a recently minted Ph.D. in some field of science and have started to think about making your first application for research funding from some external source, this book is addressed primarily to you. I believe, however, that others will also find the information provided here useful – senior scientists, graduate students, and administrators working in institutional

Sponsored Projects Offices, as well as anyone who is simply curious about how the research funding enterprise works at the ground level.

While we are in the mode of Introduction, let me introduce myself. I retired in 2001 after more than twenty-five years as a program officer at the National Science Foundation (NSF). For most of my time at NSF I directed the Linguistics Program. I also participated in numerous committees managing special cross-disciplinary programs and initiatives, spanning various parts of NSF, and in the process learned a fair amount about the wide variety of ways that NSF programs and NSF program officers work. I spent a great deal of my time answering questions from people who were preparing proposals to send to NSF, or thinking about doing so. From that experience I learned what things puzzle people the most about the proposal writing and research funding process. In a sense, this book is an organized compendium of my answers to the most frequently asked questions I received as a program officer.

Given my background, I write from a particular perspective. My career was at the NSF, and I came to know that agency well, so it naturally predominates in these pages. Some of the matters the book addresses, such as research topic selection, project planning, research ethics, and project management, are fairly generic and transcend the practices of individual funding agencies. When we come to the more specific, detailed matters such as special funding mechanisms, proposal writing, and the review process, however, the information and advice you will find here applies directly to the way things are done at the NSF, and only with modifications to other agencies. I frequently remind the reader to seek comparable information for other agencies from their Web sites or their program officers. Chapter 3 surveys the major funding agencies, with some indication of their aims and their procedures, and offers directions for finding out more about them. At a few other points in the book, I provide some agency-specific information about other agencies, primarily the National Institutes of Health (NIH).

My perspective is also shaped by my field, linguistics, and my own practices as a program officer. The fact that my training is in a particular field of science is not, in my opinion, a significant limitation on the value of the book. The basic principles of planning an effective research project and writing a good proposal do not change from one field of science to another. If there is a limitation, it stems from the fact that NSF program officers have wide latitude to run their programs in varied ways, according to the needs and traditions of their diverse research communities. Thus, a situation or practice I describe in one way in the book may in fact be handled differently in some NSF programs. I have tried to minimize the problem in two ways: by soliciting feedback on draft chapters of the book from program officers in a variety of fields (whose help I gratefully recognize in the Acknowledgments), and by liberal use of words like "usually," "normally," "typically," and so forth in passages where the description I offer applies in most cases but perhaps not all.

The book has a fundamental premise that explains its content and structure: that proposal writing is best approached not as an isolated activity, but as part of a larger process of planning and carrying out a research project. That broader view distinguishes this book from others on the topic of writing effective grant proposals. Here, "Writing a Proposal" is only one chapter out of nine (the longest one, to be sure). I maintain that planning a project thoroughly before beginning to write a proposal to fund it makes writing the proposal easier and results in a better proposal. This book will guide you through the whole process.

Now let's get started.

1

Selecting a Research Topic

Every research project begins with an idea – a question whose answer nobody knows yet, and a guess as to what that answer might be. Finding the right question to ask is often the most difficult task facing the researcher. The best scientists seem to have a knack for formulating interesting, productive research topics. Although it is probably beyond the ability of a book or a teacher to impart this skill directly, we can identify some of the distinguishing characteristics of a well-chosen research topic.

The context constrains the choice. This book is about planning and proposing research projects for funding, so that is the context we will assume here. Other contexts, such as selecting a topic for a term paper or for a lifelong pursuit, might lead to a different choice.

A good research topic successfully balances a set of desirable but conflicting goals. These goals fall into a number of opposing pairs that you can think of as the endpoints or poles of dimensions that describe the topic.

The Dimensions of Topic Selection

1. Focused vs. **Extended**. Research is an attempt to shine a beam of light into a dark place. Like a beam of light, research can be focused more or less sharply, and the choice of focus can be a key to determining how fruitful the research turns out to be.

4

The topical focus must be clear and sharp. It needs to be clear enough to make the empirical content of the research question evident, and what an answer to that question would mean. It needs to be sharp enough to indicate, not only to the investigator but also to others a logical line of research to pursue the topic – what the first steps will be, and the steps after that.

Let's consider an example. Suppose you are a cognitive scientist about to organize a new research project, and you're interested in memory. How do you formulate the research topic? What is the right degree of focus, the right level of specificity? Clearly "memory" is far too broad. So you narrow the focus successively to "human memory," "children's memory," and "development of memory in children" – all still too broad because they subsume too many different researchable questions, but getting better. Looking at the role of formal schooling in the development of memory in children is getting close, but there are still enough different things going on in school that this doesn't define the question quite sharply enough. So you zero in on research on "linking teacher talk and the development of children's memory" (which is the title of an actual research project funded by the NSF in September 2002).

But the dimension has an opposing pole to consider as well. The research topic, while focused enough to be clear, also must be broad enough to be interesting. If it is too tightly constrained, the answers that emerge from the research, however well-defined and well-grounded, will not extend to the constellation of closely related questions that interest others.

In our example, the investigator might have narrowed the focus further; say, to female children, or to teachers over 40 years old, or to teacher talk at the beginning or the end of the school day. Perhaps as the research progresses and we learn more about the topic, there will be reason to narrow the focus in these or other ways. But for this subject at this time, those restrictions would only diminish the interest of the research.

To return to the light beam metaphor, if you want to illuminate a particular patch on a wall, you are best served by a light beam that is focused to the approximate dimensions of the patch, rather than one which diffusely lights the entire wall, or another which narrowly shines on only a small portion of the patch.

It should already have become apparent that the proper point on the dimension of focus depends greatly on the particular field of research, and the current state of the art of research in that field. This is true of all of the dimensions that we will discuss, and is a point that we will return to later.

2. Novel vs. **Grounded.** There is a canard about grant funding to the effect that you can only get funded for work you've already done, that the proposal review process is too conservative to be receptive to genuinely new ideas. In fact, the opposite is closer to the truth. It is a sure death sentence to a proposal if a reviewer can demonstrate that the proposed research has already been done. Only truly novel work can make the kind of contribution to our knowledge that merits support from a funding agency or, for that matter, attention from colleagues in your field.

Novelty in the scientific sense requires more than mere difference. A proposed experiment can be different from any performed before without being novel, if the difference is not in some key variable or variables that are essential to the result. Suppose, for example, that you are studying brain responses to auditory stimuli, and you are able to determine from the literature on the topic that in all previous studies, the subjects were either seated or prone. Now you could propose to do the experiment differently by having the subjects standing; however, to make the case that this is a truly novel experiment, you will have to argue persuasively that there is some reason to believe that bodily posture plays a significant role in the neurophysiology of audition. A pilot experiment suggesting such a role could help to make the case, and perhaps that option lies behind the canard mentioned above, but there is a big difference between doing a pilot experiment to motivate undertaking a line of research and actually carrying out the research.

While research must be novel to merit attention and funding, it must at the same time be well-grounded in established scientific knowledge. The successful construction of a perpetual motion device, or of cold fusion, to take a more recent example, would certainly be novel, but inconveniently they violate known laws of physics. Reviewers would not take seriously a proposal for one of these projects unless the proposal could make a persuasive case for revisions in the physical laws. These examples are far-fetched enough, and familiar enough, to be amusing, but in fact it is all too frequent for proposals to leap so far beyond current knowledge and technique that reviewers lose confidence in the investigator's ability to carry out the research proposed.

The literature review section of a research proposal, which we will discuss more fully later, is important here, not only for the case it makes to reviewers of how well-grounded and how novel the proposed research is, but also because preparing it can help you select a research topic that is adequately grounded and still interestingly novel.

3. Feasible vs. **Challenging**. It is important to select a research topic that you can realistically undertake and complete with the time and resources available to you. This is related to the matter of groundedness. A topic has to be scientifically feasible, given the current state of the field, and a poorly grounded project is likely to be *a priori* infeasible. Beyond that, the feasibility must be practical as well. Even a project that is eminently well-grounded from a scientific point of view may not be feasible in terms of its cost, its facilities requirements, or the time it will take to carry it out. This is most commonly a problem for inexperienced investigators, who may not yet have internalized a sense of what it takes to carry out a project to completion, but it can happen on a grand scale as well, as the history and demise of the Superconducting Super Collider attest.

Of course, when you are writing a proposal for submission to a funding agency, you are requesting resources to make it possible for you to carry out a project that might be infeasible without the requested support. So the feasibility of a proposed project is contingent on receiving the funding requested, but is still an important factor in the evaluation of the proposal. Reviewers have to agree that the resources available to the investigator, including the funding requested if it is awarded, match the needs of the project. Feasibility may also be contingent on other factors, such as favorable environmental conditions, and you need to be aware of these and reflect that awareness in your proposal.

The other pole of this dimension is that the project should be a challenge to carry out, both intellectually and practically. It should lie just at the threshold of feasibility. The practical challenge ensures that you will stretch the resources and make the most effective and

productive use of them, and of your own time and effort, that is possible. The intellectual challenge will beget the most exciting results if
the project succeeds. Again, this dimension is something that reviewers will attend to in evaluating your proposal, but is also something
that you will want to get right on your own behalf, to maximize the
results of your efforts.

4. Theoretical vs. **Empirical**. A common criticism of a research
proposal that is inadequately grounded in a theoretical framework
is to call it a "fishing expedition." A proposal of this sort defines
a set of data to collect, and procedures for collecting the data, but
does not explain the purpose or the significance of the effort, other
than to characterize the phenomena to be studied as important. The
investigator apparently expects the regularities and patterns in the
data, and the significance of those patterns, to become self-evident
once the data are gathered and laid out for inspection. Experienced
scientists know that it rarely works that way. It is much more productive to approach the research problem with a theoretical model,
however tentative and incomplete, that suggests that the world is organized in a certain way, with regard to the phenomena under study.
The model will inevitably contain gaps that generate questions to
explore, and the investigator will have guesses – hypotheses – as to
the answers to the questions. These questions and hypothesized answers will provide the logical foundation for a plan of research that
has direction and purpose. Of course, the results of the research are
likely to show that the theoretical model was wrong in some way and
must be revised before generating more questions to study, but that's
progress, and a more valuable outcome than to have a collection of
data of unclear relevance or significance.

It's possible to go too far in the opposite direction, however. Research that focuses exclusively on questions internal to a formal theory, without predicting or testing their empirical consequences, is
likely to strike reviewers as sterile. There are some exceptions in fields
with a highly developed theoretical apparatus such as physics or economics (and of course, mathematics is a case of its own), but in most
fields, the empirical content of a proposed line of research needs to
be clear.

5. Near-Term Results vs. **Long-Term Prospects**. The requisites
of planning research projects to attract a funding sponsor give this

dualism its importance. The typical length of funding that an investigator, particularly a new investigator, can expect in response to a successful research proposal is two to three years – five at most. If you hope to attract further funding after that, it's essential that the first period of funding lead to some useful results. In an ideal world, there might well be superb research projects that would not yield their results before ten or more years of work. But in the world we live in, significant results must appear at more frequent intervals if funding support is to continue, and you have to take this fact of life into account in selecting a research topic. It's fine, indeed desirable, to have a long-term vision of where your research is headed, but you have to divide that long-range plan up into individual stages of a few years each that can yield valuable results on their own.

On the other hand, a topic whose possibilities you can exhaust with two or three years of research is probably too narrowly defined to interest people evaluating the proposal. An exciting research topic is one that will yield results that open up new avenues for further research – and in the process, not so incidentally, provide the basis for a later proposal for renewed support.

The Goldilocks Principle

When Goldilocks visited the house of the three bears, she tried out their food and their furniture to see how it all suited her tastes. She found one bowl of porridge too hot, another too cold, but the third one just right. She sat in a chair that was too hard, another that was too soft, and a third that was just right. Ditto for the beds.

Your task as an investigator selecting a research topic is similar to Goldilocks'. Along the various dimensions that we've just discussed, you want to find the best point to situate your own work. You want a topic that is neither too broad nor too narrow, novel but still grounded, feasible but challenging, theoretically motivated but theory-transcendent, offering both near-term results and long-term prospects. On each of these dimensions, you want what Goldilocks wanted – to find the point that is Just Right.

As we've mentioned before, the Just-Right point on each of the dimensions depends heavily on the field of research and on the state of the art in that field at the time you're planning the project. A brand-new line of research that follows up some exciting recent discovery will probably be more novel and less tightly focused than work within a paradigm that has been extensively explored. Research that depends on the use of extremely expensive equipment may allow a longer time line for useful results than research that is more personnel-intensive. And so on. Your challenge as a creative scientist is to make the right choice for your field and your time.

How do you know what the right choice is? You don't, not really, not at the beginning of research, which by its nature is an unpredictable enterprise. You find out by the results how apt the choice of topic really was. But there are things you can do to help give you the best chance to select a good topic. First, be active in your field. Go to professional meetings to hear what others are doing and discuss it with them. Keep up with the current literature. Keeping tabs on what's going on in this way helps you to know what is novel and what is familiar, and also gives you a sense for such things as the appropriate level of focus. Second, as you develop tentative ideas for a research topic, share them with others whose opinions you value. You can do this in individual conversations; sometimes an informal colloquium with colleagues is a good forum for airing your ideas. The reactions you get may indicate to you problems and possibilities that you hadn't considered, ways to improve the topic, or reasons to abandon it. You might even find a collaborator in the process. Once you have selected a topic, it is going to dominate a lot of your thought and time and effort for a good long while, so it pays to get it Just Right.

Project Scale and Duration

Deciding how much time and what resources you will devote to a project might seem to be a topic for the next chapter, on project planning, but in fact these decisions are crucial in topic selection because they constrain the choice of topic in significant ways. Moreover, external factors impose practical limits on the time and resources that you can hope to employ in your project. To a large extent, you can get a good sense of these limits while you are still in the topic selection phase of the project, and you can use that knowledge to help you zero in on a topic that fits them.

Seasoned investigators with strong track records understandably have broader latitude in the amount of time and funding that they can realistically request for a project than a freshly-minted scientist submitting a first proposal. For new researchers, the norms are fairly well established. The duration of funding that you can expect to receive is likely to be two or three years (CAREER grants, which we discuss in Chapter 4, run longer). The roster of personnel that the funding will support are a Principal Investigator, full-time during the summer and possibly part-time during the academic year; a graduate student research assistant (if you're at an institution that has grad students); and one or two undergraduates. A grant can also include funding for equipment, travel, supplies, and other expenses of research. We will return to these items in the chapter on proposal writing, but they are usually not limiting factors in topic selection in the same way that duration and staff are.

We just mentioned that the duration of a funded project is likely to be two or three years. Three-year (and longer) projects and proposals actually differ somewhat in kind from two-year projects and proposals, not just in duration, and you need to decide at the outset which kind of project you are proposing. You should request two years of funding if (1) it is reasonable to expect that the full project can be completed in that amount of time, *or* (2) the project is so open-ended that you can't foresee very clearly what you'll be doing by the time the project enters its third year. An example of the latter type of project is a highly theoretical or mathematical line of research in which each interim result opens up a whole new set of possible paths to follow, and it's difficult or impossible to predict which particular branching paths you will be on by the third year. Reviewers are unlikely to react warmly to a proposal when they have to guess what will happen after some point in the funding period. Conversely, a three-year proposal is appropriate if (1) you can lay out a clear and specific line of research for three years, *and* (2) it is reasonable to expect the full project to take at least that long. An example here is a series of laboratory experiments that explore different variables in a topical phenomenon. You can describe in advance how you will do each experiment, accurately project how long each experiment will take, and show that collectively the experiments will require three years to perform. In some fields, such as ecology, the time scales of the phenomena studied dictate projects and grants of longer duration, and here three- or four-year grants are the norm.

Bear in mind that duration is negotiable. That is, you can propose a project with a stated duration, and if the reviewers and funding agency like the project but believe that it should be funded for less (or more!) time than you have requested, the agency can offer to fund a modified form of the project. It will then be up to you to decide whether you want to undertake the project as modified. This is getting ahead of ourselves at this stage, but the point here is that you should feel free to propose the project duration you consider most appropriate for your topic without worrying that the proposed duration by itself will damage your chances for funding.

The Most Important Thing

We've tried in this chapter to help you organize and focus your thinking as you select a topic for your research. After all of the considerations of focus, novelty, feasibility, duration, and the rest, however, the single most important factor is finally your own preference. Pick a topic that excites you profoundly, a question that arouses your intense curiosity. Life is too short, and good research too difficult, to do anything else. You will write the best proposal on the topic that interests you the most, and if the proposal is funded, that is the topic that you will do the best research on. Although you need to be mindful of the overall constraints imposed by funding agencies on such matters as project duration and budget, it is a serious mistake to try to guess what the funder wants and tailor your research accordingly. Chances are the funder doesn't have that clear an idea of what will be the best work anyway, and is looking to the proposals to find out. And if you should receive a grant for doing research that you don't care passionately about, you may find carrying out the project to be a burden rather than the joy that it ought to be.

2

Project Planning

With a research topic in mind, it's time to start planning exactly how you are going to organize the project to study it. Notice that we did *not* say that it's time to start writing the research proposal. That is a strong and common temptation because the proposal is the most immediate tangible requirement facing the investigator, usually with a rapidly approaching deadline, but it is one to avoid. After careful project planning, the proposal will flow naturally and logically; but writing a proposal before working out the project plans first is an exercise in frustration and constant rewriting, as you repeatedly discover in writing a later part that you have to revise an earlier part to keep the whole thing coherent. In this chapter, we'll discuss a strategy for project planning that should give you the basis for writing a well-organized, logically coherent proposal in a limited amount of time.

Planning for Life or for a Proposal

In the first chapter, we mentioned the difference between selecting a research topic that is appropriate for a two- or three-year project and one that will occupy all or a large portion of your professional career. The same thought applies to project planning more generally. You may well have a set of long-term goals for what you want to do and to accomplish, scientifically, at various stages of your career. The kind of research planning we are discussing here, however, is both more limited and more extensive than that. It is more limited in scope and duration, focusing on the two- to three-year period for which you will be seeking funding. It is more extensive in the sense that you need to figure cut in detail, as best you can, exactly what you expect to be doing from month to month while the project is under way. It should go without saying that the immediate project you are planning should fit congenially into your longer-range plans; but it is the plan for the immediate project that will drive the proposal you will be writing.

Who You Are = How You Plan

Just as people's personalities differ, so too do their styles of planning and organizing research projects. Some folks prefer to jump head-long into a topic, start working on something that looks interesting, and then follow promising paths as they emerge. Others are more methodical and systematic, thinking out the various possible paths and contingencies in advance before starting the actual work. The latter group generally have a much easier time writing good proposals. They can provide a proposal that gives reviewers a strong idea of how the project is intended to proceed from start to finish, not just how it will begin. The reviewers know that the actual course of the project may deviate from the plan as new results open up new lines of research, but with a plausible scenario before them, they don't have to imagine one.

Although a project plan should guide rather than constrain research, there are nonetheless some extremely creative, insightful scientists who find plans and timetables a hindrance to good research rather than a help. Those people do well to team up with someone with a more structured approach in order to prepare a successful research proposal.

For most people, it's safe to say, doing the planning and organizing necessary to prepare a good proposal is a major benefit to the actual work, even if the proposal should ultimately fail to attract funding. The planning process itself can reveal problems and pitfalls that might arise during the project, and suggest ways to avoid them. It provides a mechanism for setting priorities, so that time and resources can be devoted to component parts of the project in proportion to their relative importance. The plan guides and motivates work during the periods between flashes of inspiration. And it ensures that all the members of the research team have a common understanding of what is to be done.

A Strategy for Planning

There are no doubt many different ways to develop a useful research plan, and if planning comes easily and naturally to you, you should do what works for you. As we just observed, however, there are some people for whom the process is more difficult and who could use some advice on how to go about it. If you're in this latter group, here is a strategy you can try.

The essence of the strategy is to work from the two ends of the project – the beginning and the project goals – towards the "middle." Meaning: what you know best when you start a project are (1) your present state, call it S; and (2) the project goals, call them G. The idea of the project plan is to get from S to G as efficiently as possible. So, you work backwards from G and forwards from S until you achieve continuity.

To do this, you first have to formulate S and G in precise detail. S includes the current state of your knowledge, based on your review of the literature and your own prior research; and the resources at your disposal – people, facilities, equipment, supplies, etc. G includes the intellectual and tangible outcomes you are trying to achieve.

This is easier to follow at a less abstract level, so let's explore some hypothetical examples representing different types of research in different fields of science.

Here are examples of some possible project goals: a set of chemistry experiments to determine new details about polymerization; a 5,000-word dictionary of an undescribed language; a monograph in a new area of mathematical theory; a sociological survey of 400 subjects. And let us imagine a likely pre-project state for each of these projects: three pilot projects completed to demonstrate the validity of the experimental technique; two hours' worth of transcribed texts from previous fieldwork on the language; a new idea; a survey instrument drafted.

It's worth noting, by the way, that we're assuming that a certain level of background preparation has already taken place by the time you get to the stage of actually planning the project. That's because we're discussing project planning in the context of preparing to write a research proposal for the project. Proposing a project for which you have done *no* background preparation is very unlikely to be successful.

Now, given the beginning and ending points, the task is to find an effective path between them. The balance between planning forward from the present state and backward from the project goal depends on the nature of the research.

Take the chemistry project as the first example. Suppose that you are planning a three-year project, and you know from past experience that you can complete about three experiments a year, so you are planning a series of nine experiments. You have just mastered the use of a new synthetic reaction, and have an idea that it may lead to a new way to prepare an important class of anticancer drugs. The payoff of the project, if all goes well, will be to synthesize a drug in this class, so that is the ninth experiment. To guide your planning, design that ninth experiment in as much detail as you can. This is a thought exercise at this point, of course – you can't actually do the experiment yet, or it wouldn't take you three years to get around to doing it. But in thinking about the design of the ninth experiment, you will identify a number of things that you need to know, or to do, in order to be able to carry it out. In analyzing these gaps in your current knowledge, you will find that some are logically prior to others. Some are things that you can do immediately, without further preparation; others have prerequisites of their own. With this information, you are in a position to design a cumulative sequence of experiments, starting with the ones that you can do now, and using the results of those to enable you to undertake the later ones, culminating in the ninth experiment that is the key outcome of the project, if all goes according to plan.

The dictionary project is one that can be planned forward from your present situation, for the most part. It is a matter of preparing the entries, one by one, until you have exhausted your data. The techniques for preparing the entries will remain fairly constant, and the entries fairly independent from one another, so the process is one of accumulation rather than sequencing, although some revising of earlier work is likely to be necessary in the light of later analysis. You need to plan a schedule – how many entries you intend to complete within a given amount of time – and a division of labor among the members of the research team, which could be found by dividing up the transcribed texts, or by specifying which classes of words each person will work on, or by dividing up the tasks involved in the preparation of each individual entry. However, this project also may require some planning of the overall sequence of events. You may decide, for example, that you need to do more fieldwork to be able to complete the project. When should this be done – at the start of the project, or after you have done a certain amount of the work? Should the fieldwork be devoted entirely to data gathering, or should you plan to do some analysis and compilation of entries while in the field as well?

The theoretical monograph is in some ways the most difficult sort of project to plan, because you can have only a vague idea of how it will turn out at the end. The goal you have in mind may prove to be ultimately unattainable, or you may have a brilliant insight some-where along the way that changes the whole direction of the project. These complications can happen in all types of research, of course, but they are somewhat more likely in purely theoretical work. There is still some planning to do, however. Based on your own experience from your past work, you need to make an educated guess as to how long it will take you to flesh out your current ideas and build them into a structure that is solid enough to publish, and then map out a schedule for the project. Also, this type of project usually benefits from interactions with colleagues, wrestling out with them the no-tions that you are finding difficult to deal with in some way. You should explicitly incorporate these interactions into the project plan, deciding how much of this you want or need to do, and at what stages of the overall project.

The survey research project resembles the dictionary project at the outset, in that there is a large chunk of repetitive work to do in ad-ministering the survey instrument to the full population of subjects. In this project, however, that is only the beginning; the organization, analysis, and interpretation of the data to produce interesting results may well take as much time as the data collection, or even more. The purpose of the project is to test a hypothesis, and the data are the means to that end, not an end in themselves. It is essential to incorporate adequate time for analysis into the overall project plan, to avoid the danger of coming to the end of the project with a mass of uninterpreted data. Moreover, this type of research may be more subject to external constraints than others we've been discussing because it depends on access to a large population of subjects. You have to determine not only who the subjects will be, but also when they will be available to you, and not on vacation, say, or preoccupied with matters that are more pressing to them (for example, final exams for a population of undergraduate students). Thus, the time course of a project like this needs to be more rigorously planned than for some other sorts of projects.

A planning technique you might find helpful is one that some mentors have urged on their dissertation students. Pretend that you have completed the project, and now have to draft a paper reporting the results. Write a theoretical introduction stating the research question and describe the methodology. Make up a plausible set of data, then analyze it to derive and support some conclusions. The exercise is likely to stimulate you to think about the relationships between the research question, the methodology, the data, the analysis, and the conclusions – and sharpen your plans in the process.

Timetables

In the previous chapter, we mentioned that you should already have a project duration in mind when you select the research topic. Now in the project planning stage, you have to make that decision firm, deciding on the exact length, to the month, of the project you are planning. Normally, as we said, the duration is likely to be twenty-four or thirty-six months (possibly longer in some fields). Having set the duration of the project, you then are in a position to formulate a specific project plan that fits within that duration, with a specific timetable.

The funding agency may or may not require that your proposal include a timetable, but even if it does not, the timetable is a definite asset to your planning and is something that you should prepare even if you do not end up including it in the proposal. Think of yourself as the primary audience for the timetable, and prepare it in a format and at a level of detail that will be most useful to you. There is no need to use elaborate planning tools such as PERT charts, unless you yourself find them helpful. Visualize the project as you foresee it actually unfolding in real time, breaking it down into its major components and estimating how long each of those should take; then translate that into a calendar-based sequential schedule that covers the planned duration of the project. It may prove useful to further subdivide the project and develop subschedules for the major components, if you can do that meaningfully and realistically.

The timetable is like a budget, where the currency is time rather than money. Recall that we said earlier in this chapter that project planning is a mechanism for setting priorities. It is here in the timetable that priority setting takes tangible shape. When you have set down the first draft of the timetable, you are then in a good position to study it as a whole and see if it makes sense in terms of the major aims of the project – are you dividing your research time among the major project components roughly in proportion to their relative importance to the main project goals? It's also a good time to revisit the question of feasibility – can you realistically expect to complete everything you are planning in the time available? If you find that you need to make adjustments to your plans, it's much easier to do so at this point than after you have drafted most of a proposal.

Some factors may affect your project schedule that you can't control and may simply have to adapt to. For example, the weather at a field site may make work impossible in some seasons. Subjects may not be available during school vacations. Animals may be hibernating or migrating at certain times of year. Keep such considerations in mind in setting up your project timetable. And allow for the unexpected! Research can be full of surprises, and your schedule needs to be flexible enough to deal with them without throwing the whole project off track.

Money

When you have a plan that is solid enough to give you confidence that you are prepared to undertake the project, it is time to start thinking about what it will cost. We will discuss budgeting in detail in the chapter on writing a proposal, but there is information that you will need at the time that you write the proposal budget that you should start to collect now. For example, you may need research equipment, including computers and their peripherals, that are available from several vendors. You need to contact the vendors to get price quotes, so that you can identify the most competitive price, and so that you will be in a position to specify a price in the proposal budget. If you will be working with human subjects, or consultants, or linguistic informants, you need to determine the prevailing rate of pay in the locale where you will be working. If you expect to travel as part of the project, you need to get quotes on airfares and the costs of accommodations where you will be staying. You need to estimate what expendable supplies and contracted services you will need for the project, and what they will cost.

Some project costs, such as the pay for project personnel and the institutional indirect costs, are set by the policies at your institution, and your Sponsored Projects Office (SPO) will tell you what those must be (more on this later). But much of the project budget is under your direct control, and it is your responsibility to know what the costs are, to be sure that they are reasonable and proper for the items to be purchased, and to foresee the project's material needs accurately so that you neither find yourself surprised at a cost that should have been anticipated nor prepare a budget that is inflated beyond the project's genuine needs.

The size of your budget will affect your choice of a funding source. If your project is going to cost a million dollars a year, there's no point in proposing it to a funding program whose entire annual budget is that amount or less. Nonetheless, it's better to plan the project the way you want to do it first, with the budget it requires, and then look for a funding source with resources that meet your needs (identifying funding sources is the topic of the next chapter). If it turns out that you've priced yourself out of the market, that there is nowhere you can find funding in the amounts you've envisioned, then you can begin to think about how to fit your project to the funding that's available in your field. You might scale it back to a smaller, less costly project, preserving your primary research priorities. Or you might stretch it out over more time, so that each individual year of the project costs less.

Larger Projects

We have been focusing on planning research projects of a scale that is appropriate for a single investigator with the assistance of some graduate and undergraduate students. Most readers of this book are likely to be just embarking on an independent research career, preparing to submit their first proposal on their own behalf, and that is the sort of project that they are likely to be planning. However, the government agencies that fund scientific research fund a substantial number of projects of a larger scale, with a number of investigators collaborating on a common problem, often from the perspectives of diverse disciplines. So it is perhaps worth saying a bit about the special issues involved in planning these larger projects.

The major issue in any research project involving more than one investigator is coordination. It is essential to have mechanisms in place to ensure that people are in fact working in concert toward a common goal, and that some member of the team isn't veering off on a tangent that may seem more interesting but does not contribute to the joint effort. Coordination must be built into the project planning from the very beginning. All of the collaborating researchers need to participate actively in planning the project, each making sure that the timeline for his or her own contribution is realistic and that the schedule allows ample opportunities for interaction with, and input from, the other team members as needed. Thus, if Jim needs a result from Rosalind's work before he can undertake his second experiment, the schedule has to be arranged so that there is time for Rosalind to produce that result in time for Jim's second experiment.

The project plan needs to include an explicit mechanism for monitoring coordination and progress on a regular basis. This will typically be in the form of regular meetings of the project personnel at appropriate intervals, say weekly, if all of the project personnel are in the same location. For projects that are geographically spread out, other methods using electronic communication are necessary, such as a private Web site for the project staff, e-mail, teleconferencing by telephone or video, or combinations of these modes, as well as occasional travel for face-to-face meetings. A highly multidisciplinary project may require especially high levels of interaction among the participants, as they seek to learn a common technical language, devise a comprehensive theoretical framework, and establish satisfactory research protocols. What is important is that the team explicitly select the most suitable mechanism or mechanisms at the initial stages of planning the project, and then employ them faithfully.

A larger project will also impose a larger administrative burden on the investigators, for routine matters such as ensuring that bills are paid, supplies are ordered as needed, communication and correspondence with the funding agency and other interested parties are current, project staff are in conformity with institutional personnel regulations, and so forth. Single-investigator projects have to deal with these matters as well, of course, but somehow such chores seem to multiply in a nonlinear fashion as more researchers join the team. Thus the staff for a larger project will probably require a full-time or part-time administrator in addition to the scientific personnel.

Scientists collaborating on a research project are putting their careers and their egos on the line. It is vital for the project plan to include a clear, explicit, mutually agreed-to delineation of the assignment and sharing of responsibility and authority among the project team, to avoid later arguments and recriminations that can hinder the progress of the project and engender bad feelings and relationships among the collaborators. In a similar vein, it is helpful to decide in advance how credit for the project results will be attributed, for example in the order of authorship of papers emerging from the research.

The funding agency requires that a project have one Principal Investigator (PI). The agency allows a proposal to designate some number of Co-Principal Investigators, but will regard the first-named of these as the PI, even if that title doesn't appear on the proposal. From the agency's point of view, it needs a single point of contact for communication regarding the project, and a single individual who accepts scientific and administrative responsibility for the project and any grant funds awarded to support it; being the "Principal Investigator" is not a matter of special honor or prestige as far as the funding agency is concerned. Among the scientists working on the project, however, it may be, and so the entire team should agree on who is to be the PI, and why, and be comfortable with that, to avoid hard feelings later.

Final Thoughts on Planning

Keep in mind while developing a project plan that it is just that, a *plan*, and not a blueprint or a contract. Research is too unpredictable for it to be otherwise. Circumstances may require you to deviate from it or to reformulate it. If that happens, do so consciously and deliberately, and try to revise the plan in a way that still allows meeting the ultimate goals of the project if possible.

The most common error in planning a research project is planning to do too much. A less common but still extant error is the opposite, planning to do too little. If your planning is in preparation for submitting a research proposal, you should realize that the reviewers evaluating your proposal will include experts in your type of research, and they will criticize a plan that is unrealistically ambitious in terms of the amount of work to be done in the specified time, or conversely a plan that is so leisurely that it's not clear what the investigator will be doing with his or her time. Here again, we can invoke the Goldilocks principle: you need to find the right balance, the right point on the continuum between these opposing errors.

But even aside from its bad effect on the proposal's evaluation, a too-busy plan leads to constant frustration and worry, as you inevitably fall short of the timetable; and a too-loose plan is little better than no plan at all because it gives no guidance on how well on track you are toward the project goals.

3

Identifying Funding Sources

When the research plan is well developed enough that it is time to start thinking about preparing a proposal, the first step is to decide where to submit it. That decision will significantly affect how you write the proposal, and is itself significantly constrained by the nature and scope of the research you are planning. The purpose of this chapter is to give you some practical guidance in deciding where to seek funding for your research.

U.S. Government Agencies – Missions and Methods

Since discovering in World War II how scientific knowledge could bestow military advantage, the U.S. Government has been the largest single supporter of scientific research in the world. Through its own laboratories and think tanks, and through grants and contracts to scientists based in universities and other research institutions, the U.S. Government has invested hundreds of billions of dollars in basic and applied research across the full spectrum of scientific disciplines. The government's commitment to this support has been largely free of partisan political dispute, and has continued uninterrupted through numerous changes of administration and political control of Congress. Thus any American scientist seeking research funding from outside the walls of his or her own institution has to at least consider the possibility of applying to the federal government for it.

To call the U.S. Government a "single" supporter of research, as we just did, is accurate in the sense of contrasting it with the panoply of universities, industrial laboratories, and private research labs, which collectively provide more research support from their own resources than the federal government does, although no single institution equals it. It is misleading, however, in the sense that the government is not a single entity from the point of view of the scientist who wishes to submit a proposal for funding, but rather a collection of different agencies, each with its own aims and procedures. We will devote most of this chapter to exploring the U.S. Government agencies that have been the most active in supporting basic scientific research through funding investigators who are employed by some other institution.

Every government agency has its own mission, its own purpose in the larger scheme of things. The mission can often be stated very succinctly, perhaps in just a few words, but for a big agency the interpretation of those words can be very broad indeed. Nonetheless, each agency imposes some boundaries on the activities it will undertake and support, in keeping to its mission. The researcher needs to determine which agency or agencies are appropriate potential sources for funding the research he or she is planning.

Every agency that funds research also has its own set of methods for doing so, its own rules for when to submit proposals, how to construct proposals, how proposals will be reviewed, what level of funding will be provided, how to administer funding, and what kind of reporting is required. So deciding where you will submit a proposal clearly has a large impact on what you do next.

Fortunately, in the Internet era it's much easier than it used to be to find out what you need to know to decide where you will send your proposal, and what that decision entails in proposal preparation and submission. Every agency has its own site on the World Wide Web, and the sites provide extensive information about agency missions and procedures as well as helpful hints for proposal preparation, directories of agency staff to contact for further information, and so on. Each Web site has its own address, called a Universal Resource Locator or URL. Appendix B lists a number of agency URLs that are current at the time of writing. Web sites and URLs change faster than books do, however, so some of them may be out-of-date by the time you try to use them, and you will have to employ your Web-surfing skills to track down the information you want.

The National Science Foundation

There are two good reasons why we put the NSF at the top of the list. First, for basic science in many disciplines, it is the agency of choice for seeking funding, because it defines its mission in terms of scientific excellence rather than a particular national goal such as defense or health. Second, it is the agency that I know best, the one where I spent my career.

The U.S. Government established the NSF during the years just after the Second World War, when it became clear to the nation's political leadership that some of the Allied Forces' key military assets during that struggle – most notably the atomic bomb, but also many other things such as radar and the proximity fuze – were only possible because of basic scientific research that had taken place before the war ever started, primarily in universities. This was work that the pre-war government wasn't even aware of, wouldn't have understood if it had been aware, and wouldn't have supported if it had understood. The logical conclusion was that it was in the nation's strategic interest for the government to take on an active role in promoting and supporting scientific research, even if its outcome was uncertain and its content largely unintelligible to anyone except those who themselves were capable of doing the research.

The NSF became the one government agency with the mission to support science for its own sake, rather than as a means to some predetermined end. And it was able to adopt the important and novel principle of deciding how best to pursue its mission and expend its resources on the basis of expert advice from the community receiving the support, with a minimum of political direction. Half a century later, these are still NSF's guiding principles, although the way it implements them has evolved considerably.

NSF is organized along disciplinary lines, in a three-level hierarchy. At the top level seven Directorates represent broad areas of science, like Geosciences or Biological Sciences, as well as Engineering and Education. Each Directorate has a number of Divisions, such as Chemistry, Physics, Astronomical Sciences, and so on. There are also a few "Offices" here and there to complicate things, but we don't need to go into that level of detail here.

The organizational level that matters to the individual scientist dealing with NSF is the third one, Programs. Each NSF Program focuses on a single discipline or subdiscipline, or some particular topic that is the subject of study from different disciplinary perspectives. Some current examples of Programs are Geophysics, Economics, Galactic Astronomy, Linguistics, Sensory Systems, and Human-Computer Interaction. The Programs are NSF's synaptic connections to the scientific communities it supports. The job of the program officers who run them is to keep in constant touch with the people and the research in their respective fields, so that they know who is doing what. They represent NSF to their scientific community, and their community within NSF. The program officer will be your first and usually your only point of contact with NSF.

To find out where you and your work fit best into the NSF structure, a good way to begin is on the NSF Web site. The home page has several useful things you can do. You can identify an area of science to check out, starting at the broadest level, Directorates, and drilling down to Divisions and then to Programs. Or you can bring up a menu of general information useful to Principal Investigators. You can search through NSF publications (probably not too useful when you're just starting to learn about the agency). If you're someone who prefers to read something you can hold in your hand and mark up, and you have the paper to spare, you can print out the "Guide to Programs," a book-sized document that gives a good narrative description of the full current range of funding activities at NSF.

Some types of work that many scientists do are excluded from NSF support. To quote from the first page of NSF's *Grant Proposal Guide*: "NSF does not normally support technical assistance, pilot plant efforts, research requiring security classification, the development of products for commercial marketing, or market research for a particular project or invention, [or] research with disease-related goals, including work on the etiology, diagnosis or treatment of physical or mental disease, abnormality, or malfunction in human beings or animals."

If after studying the NSF Web site you're still not sure whether your project is appropriate to propose to NSF or not, the next step is to identify a program officer who seems to be reasonably close to your research area, and contact that person, describing your plans and asking how and where they fit within NSF (actually, that's good advice for any funding agency). Most program officers prefer to receive queries of this sort by e-mail, but you should include a telephone number where the program officer can reach you if he or she decides it would be easier to discuss your questions by phone.

The Web site's search function will take you to a staff directory, which you can search by organizational unit until you find a Program, and a program officer, that sounds like a good choice. If you pick the wrong one, not to worry, the program officer you contact will be happy to forward your inquiry on to the best person to answer it.

A growing portion of NSF grant money goes to support interdisciplinary research. The regular disciplinary Programs are hospitable to proposals that cross disciplinary boundaries, but to offer further encouragement and support to such efforts, the agency also regularly mounts special initiatives that link disparate areas of science into collaborative work on certain broad topics. Initiatives come and go, and usually don't become part of the permanent NSF organizational structure. While they are in effect, however, they can be a significant source of funding for the areas of science that they relate to, sometimes exceeding the amounts that the disciplinary Programs themselves can provide. You therefore need to be aware of what NSF initiatives are currently active, and how they relate to your own work. You can find out about them first from the NSF Web site, which lists them under the rubric of "crosscutting programs," and then from a program officer in your area. We will discuss initiatives further in the next chapter, and give some examples.

The NSF awards most of its research funding in response to "unsolicited proposals," which in governmentspeak means proposals that investigators submit on their own initiative, not in response to a formal "request for proposals" of the kind that is used when the government wants to procure a pencil or a truck or a nuclear submarine. The proposals undergo merit review, in which the opinions of expert peers of the proposals' author(s) play a major role. For the proposals emerging from the review process with the highest ratings, the NSF awards grants to support the research – grants as distinct from contracts, another type of funding mechanism the government often uses. At NSF, program officers manage the review process; make the primary decisions as to which proposals to fund, based on the outcome of the review; and administer the active grants. A large part of the remainder of this book will be devoted to the details of how to prepare a proposal, how a proposal is reviewed, and how grants work, with special reference to the NSF, so we won't go into further detail at this point.

The National Institutes of Health

The contributions of science to the national interest have been about as evident in the realm of medicine as in military technology. Numerous diseases and accidental traumas that only a generation or two ago would have killed or maimed can now be prevented or cured, as a direct result of scientific research. The government has thus been willing to sustain a long-term major commitment to funding biomedical research. Most of this funding has been channeled through the National Institutes of Health (NIH).

Note the term "Institutes." The plural form of this word is important to understanding how NIH works. The NIH is actually a confederation of twenty-seven different Institutes and Centers. The Institutes are semiautonomous agencies devoted to particular diseases (such as the National Cancer Institute) or organs (like the National Eye Institute) or life stages (for example, the National Institute on Aging). They cooperate administratively, and interact as necessary in the review of proposals and support of research, but each Institute has its own individual mission, traditions, authority structure, and political constituency. The kind of research that you're doing will determine the Institute(s) that you deal with, and you'll need to become familiar with that set of people and procedures. In the space that we have here, we will limit ourselves to discussing what is common to all of NIH, from the point of view of the external applicant for research funding, and how to find more specific information via the Internet.

On its Web site, the NIH defines its mission as "science in pursuit of fundamental knowledge about the nature and behavior of living systems and the application of that knowledge to extend healthy life and reduce the burdens of illness and disability." It goes on to say, the NIH provides leadership and direction to programs designed to improve the health of the nation by conducting and supporting research: in the causes, diagnosis, prevention, and cure of human diseases; in the processes of human growth and development; in the biological effects of environmental contaminants; in the understanding of mental, addictive and physical disorders; in directing programs for the collection, dissemination, and exchange of information in medicine and health, including the development and support of medical libraries and the training of medical librarians and other health information specialists.

In adhering to its mission, the NIH supports a great deal of basic research with no obvious immediate clinical application, but it is the responsibility of anyone who requests funding from the NIH to demonstrate how the proposed project relates to and contributes to the overall goal of improving the health of the nation.

Unlike the NSF, the NIH supports an active intramural research program in addition to funding investigators working elsewhere. Each of the Institutes maintains a number of active laboratories, with research scientists working there as employees of the U.S. Government. These are top-flight, world-class research labs; five of their scientists have received the Nobel Prize. About 10 percent of the total NIH budget supports intramural research.

NIH also differs from NSF in formally separating the review process from the funding process for supporting extramural research. The NIH has established an apparatus for initial review of all the research proposals it receives, housed in the Center for Scientific Review (CSR). The review procedure is organized along disciplinary lines, but cuts across the Institute structure to some extent. The CSR appoints distinguished external scientists to a set of study sections (also known as Scientific Review Groups, or SRGs), clustered into Integrated Review Groups (IRGs).[1] An IRG represents an area of biomedical science, and its component SRGs more specific subareas within that area. For example, the IRG for Endocrinology and Reproductive Science has five SRGs: Biochemical Endocrinology,

---

[1] It is customary to apologize for the use of acronyms, but they are common currency among the professionals in the research funding world so it is probably to your advantage to become familiar with some of the most significant or frequently used ones. In this book we will give the full expansion of each one on its first introduction, and also provide a glossary of acronyms as Appendix A.

Endocrinology, Human Embryology and Development, Reproductive Biology, and Reproductive Endocrinology.

For each SRG there is an SRA, a Scientific Review Administrator, who manages the proposal submission and review processes. The SRA also identifies and recruits the scientists who serve on the SRG, and organizes the three annual meetings of the SRG. NIH's Web site includes lists of the SRAs responsible for each of the study sections, along with contact information. It also provides current rosters of study section members – invaluable information to have if you have a good idea which SRG will review your NIH proposal. The SRA's responsibility for a proposal ends when the SRG completes its review.

NIH also has program officers, who are attached to individual Institutes. The program officers manage the funding process. Their role in making funding decisions varies by Institute. In some Institutes they function very much like NSF program officers, making funding choices that are heavily informed by, but not dictated by, the outcome of the SRG review. In other Institutes the review results entirely determine the funding decisions, which the program officers implement. Anywhere in NIH, however, your primary contact will almost always be with a program officer. The program officer will provide the advice you need while planning your application, and when you are preparing and submitting a proposal, and will inform you of the results when the review is completed. You can find listings of NIH program officers, and contact information for them, on the Web sites of the individual Institutes.

Each of the NIH Institutes has its own Advisory Council, which constitutes a second stage in the review process. The Council is a group of people not employed by the government, appointed to the Council for a specified period of time. They are primarily scientists, but may also include nonscientists who have a particular interest in the activities of the Institute. The Web pages for each Institute include a roster of the current membership of its Advisory Council. The Council meets two or three times a year to review, approve, and sometimes amend the recommendations the SRGs make.

Without going into great detail, it is worth describing briefly how the two-stage review and decision process at NIH works. A proposal arriving at NIH is assigned on the basis of its content to an IRG, and within that, to a study section (SRG). At the time of initial assignment, the Institute that would be most appropriate to fund the proposal if it is successful is also identified. The NIH notifies the applicant right away of the IRG/SRG and Institute assignment, and the applicant has the opportunity to question the assignment if he or she wishes (alternatively, the applicant can request a specific assignment at the time of submitting the proposal). NIH gives serious consideration to such a request, although it has the ultimate say.

The SRG reviews the proposal at its next meeting, and assigns it a priority score by a vote of the full committee after hearing detailed reviews of the proposal that selected SRG members have written. After the SRG meeting, the priority score is compared with the scores of all of the other proposals reviewed at that and recent meetings, and converted into a percentile ranking. The SRA forwards the proposal with the review results to the appropriate Institute, whose program officers take over responsibility for it.

When the Institute's Advisory Council next meets, it considers the proposal (along with all the others on its agenda) both in terms of its scientific quality – as evidenced by the results of the SRG review – and its potential for making an important contribution to the mission of the Institute. The Council then recommends which proposals should be funded, and at what level of funding. The Council's actions normally track the SRG recommendations very closely, but can deviate from them if there is a reason to do so. After the Council meets, the proposal goes – along with the SRG review, the Council recommendation, and the program officer's recommendation – to the Institute Director, who makes the final decision whether to fund the project.

A couple of important shortcuts to this general process should be noted. After the SRG members have written their reviews of the proposals on their agenda, but before the SRG meeting, the SRA solicits their opinions as to which proposals are likely to rank in the bottom half of the proposals on the agenda. Integrating their responses yields a list of proposals to be "streamlined," meaning that the SRG will not discuss or score them at the meeting. The applicant will receive the written reviews as feedback, but the proposal will not be part of the set sent forward to an Institute Council for consideration for funding.

There may also be expedited action on the top proposals reviewed at the meeting, that is, the ones receiving the highest priority scores. When an Institute employs this procedure, a designated subcommittee of its Advisory Council considers those proposals well in advance of the next regular meeting of the Council, and typically approves them for immediate funding.

The NIH Web site provides a number of excellent resources for someone writing an NIH proposal. In keeping with their independence, the various Institutes each provide their own guidance on their own Web sites, but the guide that has proven the most popular and the most generally useful is a set of online tutorials from the National Institute of Allergy and Infectious Diseases (NIAID).

Thanks to its widely perceived contributions to the nation's well-being, the NIH is one of the government agencies most favored by the U.S. Congress, across party and ideological lines, and the agency's funding reflects this. The NIH has an annual budget of four to five times the size of the NSF's. If your research is in the biomedical sciences, in the broad sense in which NIH defines its mission, then you have to regard the NIH as the most likely source of funding for your work.

An excellent book on research funding is *The Research Funding Guidebook: Getting It, Managing It, and Renewing It*, by Joanne B. Ries and Carl G. Leukefeld, published by Sage Publications in 1998. Ries and Leukefeld primarily address the NIH funding model, with some attention to NSF. The book concentrates on proposal writing, response to declinations, management of funded projects, and renewal strategies. Anyone considering applying to NIH for funding would profit from studying this book.

Department of Defense (DOD)

As we mentioned earlier, the U.S. Government's commitment to support of basic scientific research stemmed originally from recognizing its long-term potential for enhancing the nation's military strength. The military forces themselves, however, have long seen value in sponsoring research and development with a more immediate contribution to military needs than general basic science usually offers. In addition to running a number of research laboratories of its own, the Department of Defense supports a substantial amount of extramural research in universities and other research institutions. Like the NIH, the DOD will support basic research, but only if the relevance of the research to the Department's mission of national defense is clear.

If the Institutes of the NIH act like independent entities to some extent, the components of the DOD are even more so, basically operating as separate, distinct agencies. Each of the branches of service – Army, Navy, and Air Force – has its own research arm, including intramural labs and extramural funding programs, and there is also a research agency operating directly under the aegis of the DOD central command, thus responsible to all of the branches and to none of them. In what follows we will discuss each of these four agencies in turn, but first some general comments about the operational styles and funding mechanisms they hold in common.

The DOD research agencies differ from NSF and NIH in some fundamental ways:

1. They make a much sharper distinction between basic and applied research, with separate budgets for each category and separate rules and procedures for funding each category. The DOD's definition of "basic research" is quite narrow. What the DOD classifies as "applied research" includes a significant amount of work that NSF or NIH would support as basic science.

2. Their program officers act as "strong managers," with less reliance on external peer review of proposals than NSF and NIH employ. DOD program managers identify a research need in their area of competence, and then identify a researcher or team of researchers who can meet that need. Once in a while an unsolicited proposal will fill the bill, but usually the program managers invite researchers of their choice to submit a proposal. They ask scientists within the DOD to review the proposal, and if it passes muster, they make the funding available to do the work, subject to the approval of their superiors.

3. They fund research projects more often through contracts than through grants, with a greater degree of managerial involvement and oversight over the funded project than NSF or NIH normally exercise.

4. They provide a higher funding amount per supported project overall, although the largest differences are in research the DOD defines as "applied" rather than "basic."

5. The research they fund may be classified and thus subject to strict legal restrictions on dissemination of results and descriptions of the nature of the research. This is extremely rare for research funded by NSF or NIH.

6. They may impose more stringent restrictions on who may serve as an investigator on a funded project, such as U.S. citizenship or clearance to receive and work with classified information, depending on the nature of the research.

7. DOD funders expect and arrange for a great deal more interaction among the investigators they support than other agencies do. Periodic meetings of all of the scientists supported by a given DOD program are a regular feature of life for anyone doing research with DOD support.

The DOD funding agencies, like the NSF and the NIH, maintain Web sites with essential information about their programs and their procedures. Here we will just point out highlights for each agency. For more specific information, you should visit their Web sites.

Air Force Office of Scientific Research (AFOSR). In alphabetical first place is the AFOSR, which manages both the intramural Air Force Research Laboratory and the extramural research that the U.S. Air Force supports. The AFOSR's programs fall into four general categories: aerospace and materials sciences; physics and electronics; chemistry and life sciences (including cognition and perception); and mathematics (including computer science) and space sciences. Like each of the service branch research funding agencies, the AFOSR publishes a basic document called a "Broad Agency Announcement," or BAA, that gives details about its funding programs, including the names of its program managers and contact information for them. You can link to the BAA from the home page of the AFOSR Web site.

Army Research Office (ARO). The ARO is an office within the Army Research Laboratory (ARL), which also manages the Army's own research labs and facilities. The ARO is responsible for the extramural research that the Army supports in academic and other research institutions. Its useful Web site lists the eight general areas of science that the Army supports, with an opportunity to connect to further information about each area. The Divisions are Chemical Sciences,

Life Sciences, Physics, Materials Science, Electronics, Mathematics, Computing and Information Sciences, and Mechanical and Environmental Sciences.

The most important information for the prospective applicant is in the BAA for the ARO. The BAA lists the specific research areas that ARO will support, and names a Technical Point of Contact (TPOC – equivalent to a program officer) for each, with an e-mail address and a telephone number. It also describes the application procedures, encouraging applicants to make preliminary inquiries to the appropriate TPOC before submitting a formal proposal or a "white paper" describing research plans.

One of the research areas listed in the BAA for the ARO is "Human Research and Engineering," but a separate organization funds most of the Army-supported research in this area, which we describe next.

Army Research Institute (ARI). The full name of this Army agency is the "U.S. Army Institute for the Behavioral and Social Sciences." It sponsors basic research on training and learning; leadership; human resource practices; social structures; and cognition. It has its own Web site and its own BAA, describing areas of interest, application procedures, review procedures, proposal structure, and contact information.

Office of Naval Research (ONR). The ONR sponsors basic and applied scientific research, and advanced technological development, in support of the mission of the U.S. Navy. About a third of its budget funds the work of the Navy's own laboratories and another quarter supports researchers based in universities and non-profit research institutions (the remainder of the budget goes to private industry). ONR supports basic research in the general areas of information, electronics, and surveillance; ocean, atmosphere, and space; engineering, materials, and physical science; and human systems (medical, cognitive, neural, and biomolecular).

The Web site for ONR provides a list of its departments and divisions, organized along disciplinary lines. For each unit listed, you can link to further information, including descriptions of the area and further link-lists for the individual programs in it. The ONR does not give the names of its program officers on the relevant Web pages, but it provides a telephone number and a blind e-mail address to allow you to contact them, which you should definitely do before submitting a proposal.

There are a number of different BAAs on the ONR Web site, but "ONR's Main BAA" is the one that will be relevant to most researchers. This is a fairly succinct document that gives format and content requirements for proposals submitted to ONR, describes their evaluation procedures, and provides information about award administration and other pertinent topics. Elsewhere on the Web site you can find some informal, user-friendly advice on how to write a good proposal and how to submit it to ONR.

The ONR differs in some respects from the other DOD agencies. It tends to award grants rather than contracts for basic research, and is unlikely to fund classified projects in its support of basic research or to impose citizenship restrictions on PIs.

Defense Advanced Research Projects Agency (DARPA). Independent of the separate service branches, reporting directly to the central leadership of the DOD, is the Defense Advanced Research Projects Agency, or DARPA (the "D" has come and gone a couple of times over the years, but is currently attached). DARPA's mission is to extend the boundaries of science and technology to anticipate and meet the long-term needs of the U.S. military.

An essay titled "DARPA Over the Years," appearing on DARPA's Web site, offers a remarkably clear and candid view of the agency and its role. It's tempting to reproduce the entire essay here, but the first paragraph will give the flavor:

The Defense Advanced Research Projects Agency (DARPA) was established in 1958 as the first U.S. response to the Soviet launching of Sputnik. Since that time DARPA's mission has been to assure that the U.S. maintains a lead in applying state-of-the-art technology for military capabilities and to prevent technological surprise from her adversaries. The DARPA organization was as unique as its role, reporting directly to the Secretary of Defense and operating in coordination with, but completely independent of, the military research and development (R&D) establishment. Strong support from the senior DoD management has always been essential since DARPA was designed to be an anathema to the conventional military and R&D structure and, in fact, to be a deliberate counterpoint to traditional thinking and approaches.

The full essay (just two to three pages long) is worth reading, especially for anyone contemplating applying to DARPA for research funding.

Organizationally, DARPA is divided into a number of Offices, which reflect components of DARPA's mission rather than scientific disciplinary hierarchies. DARPA's Web site lists and describes the Offices. For each Office on the list there is a link to its own Web pages for further information, including lists and descriptions of the individual programs or research areas that the Office currently supports, along with contact information for each one.

DARPA changes its programs and the kinds of projects it supports more often than the other funding agencies we've been discussing, in keeping with its intent to stay on the leading edge of science and technology, where the world changes rapidly. It ensures this flux by rotating its program managers and its Director after terms of two to four years, and by limiting the length of any single project to five years. This pattern makes it even more essential than at other agencies to communicate with a program manager before beginning to prepare a proposal, or even a preproposal statement of research plans. The program manager can not only tell you whether and where a particular research idea is likely to find a home in DARPA, but can also provide necessary guidance on the application procedures. The DARPA Offices do publish BAAs, which can be found on the Web site, but these are not as clear and helpful as other agencies offer.

DARPA has scored some significant accomplishments in pursuing its mission, and not only in the advanced technological capabilities that the U.S. armed forces employ today. It supported the research leading to the fundamental concepts that made possible the Internet, which first came to life as the ARPAnet.

Other Government Agencies

The NSF, NIH, and DOD agencies award the majority of funding that the U.S. Government provides for scientific research at universities and other research institutions, but not all of it. Other government agencies also maintain grant programs, some fairly substantial, to support research projects in their particular areas of interest, in response to proposals submitted by investigators. To name a few, the

Department of Agriculture's National Research Initiative Competitive Grants Program awards about $100 million a year for agricultural research; the Department of Energy grants over $500 million a year through its Office of Science Financial Assistance Program for research relating to energy, especially nuclear energy; the National Security Agency has a Mathematical Sciences Grants Program that supports mathematicians to the tune of $3 million a year; and the Department of Justice, through its National Institute of Justice, provides over $50 million a year for research in criminology and forensic science. The Environmental Protection Agency and the National Aeronautics and Space Administration are also major supporters of research in areas that relate to their missions.

There are several ways you can find out about government programs relevant to your own field of research. Your professional society or association probably maintains that information and is eager to disseminate it. The librarian at your institution is trained and skilled at finding this sort of information for you. And you can undertake your own search using the tools available on the Internet. In the latter category, one essential tool is the Catalog of Federal Domestic Assistance (CFDA), maintained by the U.S. Government. This is a compendium of the many different kinds of grants and payments the federal government offers for all sorts of purposes. You can purchase a printed version from the Government Printing Office, but the Internet version is free, immediately available, and much easier to use.

The CFDA's Web site is fairly well organized and accessible to first-time users, but it has the inescapable problem of having to present an overabundance of information. Every kind of grant and loan that the government makes for any purpose, from Indian Arts and Crafts Development to the National School Lunch Program to Safety Incentive Grants for Use of Seatbelts, has its place in the CFDA lists. It can be hard to find the particular entries that are useful to you. Here are some navigational hints to get you started. On the home page, select "Find Assistance Programs." On the screen that comes up next, select "By Functional Area." This opens a page listing 20 functional areas you can link to, of which one is "Science and Technology." The screen that comes up divides this area into three subcategories: "Research – General," "Research – Specialized," and "Information and Technical." This division is rather arbitrary and not very useful, so you really need to look through all three of them.

Each of the subcategories gives a list of programs, showing the title of the program, the agency that sponsors it, and its CFDA number, the latter being the link to a separate page with details on that particular program. To avoid confusion, we should note here that CFDA uses the term "program" in a broader sense than we have been using it in this book: in the CFDA context, an entire NSF Directorate constitutes a "program," for example.

Most of the programs that fund scientific research appear in the "Science and Technology" functional area of the CFDA, but not all. The National Institute of Justice program mentioned above, for example, appears in the functional area "Law, Justice, and Legal Services." So it pays to explore other functional areas that look as though they might be relevant to your interests. There is a lot of cross-listing, with individual programs listed under different functional areas that pertain to them.

In many cases, it is possible for different government agencies to cooperate in supporting your project, if it falls within their varied spheres of interest. They can do this either directly, by each giving you a grant covering a part of the project, or indirectly, with another agency transferring funds to the one that is awarding you the grant. It will be up to the program officers at the agencies involved to make the arrangements for joint funding if they decide it's warranted, but you can take the first step by submitting your proposal to all the agencies that will accept it for review, unless there are rules that preclude it in your case (for example, NSF will not review most proposals in biological sciences simultaneously with NIH).

Private Foundations

Diverse as they are, the government agencies that fund scientific research are a model of uniformity compared to the private foundations. There are some 70,000 officially recognized private foundations in the United States. Who recognizes them? The Internal Revenue Service, who establishes the rules that they must follow. The rules relate primarily to financial management, and only in very vague, general terms to substantive activities and procedures.

A great many of the foundations are simply vehicles by which particular individuals organize their charitable giving, and do not entertain and will not accept proposals. Many others are devoted to social improvement, to the arts, or to education. A limited number support scientific research, mainly in biomedical fields, with some also active in anthropology, archaeology, and geography. If a large foundation decides to commit substantial funds to a new initiative in some area of science, it will typically go to considerable lengths to publicize that fact among the relevant research communities, so if you are someone in a position to take advantage of it, the chances are good that you will hear about it.

For these reasons, it is usually not fruitful for most researchers to devote a lot of time to exploring the funding opportunities in the world of private foundations. If you wish to explore them anyway, there are some resources to help you do so. Here again your local librarian can be very helpful. Also, at some institutions the Development Office or Sponsored Projects Office maintains information on private foundation support that may be of value to their faculties and research staff. A national non-profit organization called The Foundation Center serves as a repository of information about all of the private foundations in the United States, and devotes its efforts to disseminating that information in a variety of different ways.

The Foundation Center maintains offices in Atlanta, Cleveland, New York, San Francisco, and Washington, D.C., where anyone can go to use their computers to search their comprehensive database and to get advice from the professionals on the staff. They also have affiliated Cooperating Collections in all fifty states and Puerto Rico, libraries that maintain a core collection of informational materials for people seeking grants from private foundations. Online, The Foundation Center has a Web site that provides a lot of useful information, including where to find their offices and their Cooperating Collections. They also sell access to their database online, by monthly or annual subscription. Subscribing would rarely be a worthwhile expense for an individual researcher, but it might be a service an institutional library would provide.

There is also a free but more limited resource called Foundations On-Line. This Web site provides a list of links to about ninety of the nation's largest private foundations, each link taking you to that foundation's own Web site.

Strategies for Identifying Funding Sources

In this chapter we've taken a sort of Yellow Pages approach to finding an appropriate place to send your proposal. We've mentioned a number of different agencies, indicated the kind of research they tend to support, and suggested that you explore likely-looking ones in more detail, including talking to program officers. There are more targeted strategies that you can use, however.

Networking can give you good leads to funding sources that are active in your field of science, or are on the verge of becoming so. Your colleagues and mentors, at your own institution and elsewhere, may have valuable information that they will share with you, derived from their own efforts to seek funding, their service as reviewers or panelists for funding agencies, or simply something they heard on the grapevine.

One of the many ways your institution's *Sponsored Projects Office* (SPO) can help you is by pointing you to likely places to seek funding for your research. Part of the SPO's job is to keep track of new programs the funding agencies announce, as well as their ongoing programs, so the SPO can be a comprehensive and up-to-date source of useful advice.

Another good place to look is in the *acknowledgments* page or footnotes of books and journal articles in your field. It is customary for investigators to acknowledge the funding agency that supported their research when they publish the results of the research, and if an agency supported someone else who works in the same general area that you do, it may be a possible funding source for you as well.

4

Special Funding Mechanisms

If you convened a focus group of people experienced in the world of funding scientific research and asked them for a basic definition of the term "grant," you'd probably come up with something like the following: a sum of money awarded to an institution to enable one or two investigators to work for two or three years on a particular scientific question, the award being based on an evaluation of the scientific merits of a research proposal. At one time that was the model for the overwhelming majority of the grants from the government agencies we surveyed in the previous chapter, and it is the model that is implicit in a lot of the discussion in this book.

In recent years, however, the funding agencies, especially the NSF, have incorporated some additional policy objectives into their funding activities and have instituted some special funding mechanisms to help reach those objectives. We will explore some of those mechanisms in this chapter, concentrating on the NSF, but with some attention to the NIH as well.

The special mechanisms have varying purposes. Some aim at supporting particular groups of researchers – such as new investigators, or women, or members of ethnic minority groups that are under-represented in the community of active researchers – in an effort to enlarge and diversify that community. Others present opportunities for support of alternative models of research management, such as large multi-investigator centers or industry–university collaboration. Some emphasize particular scientific topics that have current priority for social or political reasons that go beyond science. Still others provide flexibility for program officers to meet special needs in their fields.

For some of the special funding mechanisms, the agencies set aside a portion of their budgets for funding them. In these cases there is usually a special separate protected competition, with its own announcement, procedures, and deadlines. Others are funded within the budgets allocated to the regular funding programs, and proposals addressed to them compete with the other proposals the program considers.

Let's make the discussion more concrete by examining some specific examples. A good place to start is the NSF Web site. One of the program areas listed on the home page is labeled "Crosscutting." That link takes you to a page with a long list of crosscutting interdisciplinary programs, crosscutting in the sense that they are supported by multiple Directorates at NSF, or by NSF jointly with other agencies. We'll take a look at a number of items on the list, organizing our discussion according to the different categories of purposes mentioned above.

Programs for Particular Groups of Researchers

CAREER. The CAREER program (full name: the Faculty Early Career Development Program) has become a major mechanism for NSF's support of young science faculty – people with a doctoral degree who are based in an academic institution, in a tenure-track (or equivalent) position, but still untenured. Its usage varies across NSF Directorates – in some Directorates virtually all of the grants to people in the eligible group are CAREER awards, while others use it more sparingly – but the awards are available in every field of science.

The characteristics that distinguish CAREER awards from regular grants start with their size and duration – they are five-year grants, with a minimum funding level that is higher than an average regular grant. Also, the NSF publicly identifies them as its "most prestigious awards for new faculty members." But the primary distinction is the emphasis they place on education, on integrating the teaching and research activities of the faculty members supported. A CAREER proposal must include a section on the applicant's career development plan, in addition to the five-year research plan. The career development section presents a specific description of the educational activities the applicant will engage in during the course of the grant, and how those will integrate with the research. The career development plan plays a significant role in the evaluation of the proposal and the decision to fund.

CAREER is somewhat unusual among NSF programs in that it is NSF-wide, with a uniform set of rules and a common deadline across all of the NSF Directorates, but the proposals are reviewed and the grants funded by the individual NSF Directorates, Divisions, and Programs, in competition with the other proposals they receive. NSF does not set aside a separate budget for CAREER awards, but expects each of the organizational units to make a significant number of them.

There are two reasons for the uniform aspects of the CAREER program, which relate to NSF's identification of it as "most prestigious." NSF announces all of the winners of CAREER awards in a single, well-publicized press release each year. And it selects its nominees for the PECASE award, the Presidential Early Career Awards for Scientists and Engineers, from among the winners of CAREER grants. PECASE is a governmentwide program to recognize and honor the nation's most outstanding young scientists and engineers each year. These considerations create a need for common criteria of excellence, and a common schedule for the review process, even though it may differ from the normal schedules for some parts of NSF.

ADVANCE. Despite some gains in recent years, women are still underrepresented in the science and engineering workforce, comprising less than 25 percent of the force. NSF's ADVANCE program ("Increasing the Participation and Advancement of Women in Academic Science and Engineering Careers") aims to help remedy the situation. ADVANCE is an umbrella covering a few different funding competitions, which change from time to time. At this writing there are three competitions under ADVANCE: Fellows Awards, Institutional Transformation Awards, and Leadership Awards. Briefly, the Fellows Awards provide support for individuals whose careers have been interrupted or impeded by family responsibilities or other factors that can limit the careers of women scientists and engineers, but who are now in a position to undertake full-time active research with the support of the fellowship. The Institutional Transformation Awards support academic institutions in efforts to improve the institutional climate for women scientists and engineers. The Leadership Awards recognize and support the efforts of individuals and groups involved in activities to increase the participation and advancement of women in science and engineering.

Men are eligible to apply for these awards as well as women, and may actually be competitive for the Institutional Transformation and Leadership Awards. For the Fellows Awards, however, one of the review criteria for proposals is the likelihood that the award will lead to academic career advancement of one or more women in science and engineering, and it takes some imagination to construct a situation in which a male applicant could meet that test.

NSF is committed to supporting women scientists through its regular grants, and for most women a regular research proposal will be the method of choice to apply for NSF support. For those individuals who meet the eligibility criteria and have a good case for support in line with the purposes of the programs, however, the ADVANCE programs are worth considering. Each of the ADVANCE programs runs one competition annually, with a set deadline. The ADVANCE programs have their own budgets and run their own review.

Minority Research Planning Grants and Career Advancement Awards. Another category of NSF grants designed to help enhance the diversity of the scientific workforce are the Minority Research Planning Grants (MRPGs) and Career Advancement Awards (MCAAs). These awards are designed to encourage and enable people from minority groups that are underrepresented in the U.S. science and engineering workforce to begin and advance active research careers. The Program Announcement lists the eligible minority groups as Black, American Indian, Alaskan Native (Eskimo or Aleut), Hispanic, or Native Pacific Islander.

The MRPGs and MCAAs are administered through the regular NSF program structure. The individual disciplinary programs review the proposals they receive, and consider them for funding in competition with the other proposals they review. There is no budget set aside specifically for MRPGs and MCAAs; the individual programs fund them out of their regular budgets. The MRPG and MCAA proposals follow the regular review schedules of the programs that review them, with no NSF-wide deadlines.

The MRPGs are small grants (currently under $18,000) for researchers with no previous research funding from the federal government, to enable them to undertake preliminary studies and other activities in order to prepare a competitive regular research proposal. The MCAA is a larger grant (up to $60,000 including equipment needs), for experienced investigators who have had prior research funding, to enable them to devote a year to activities that will enhance their career in some way, such as acquiring expertise in a new area or undertaking pilot work to determine the feasibility of a new line of research.

Again, NSF encourages minority researchers to apply for regular research grants, and expects to support them primarily in that way, but in some cases these special mechanisms may be helpful. It's essential to talk with a program officer in your field to get a sense of whether you would be better advised to apply for a regular grant or for an MRPG or MCAA.

Alternative Models of Managing Research and Education

Science and Technology Centers (STC). The regular grant, on the model described at the beginning of this chapter, has proven to be an extremely effective way to support scientific research across a broad spectrum of disciplines. There are questions and problems in science, however, that go beyond the scope of what one or two investigators can hope to deal with in the space of a few years. Some very productive research areas require teams of researchers from diverse disciplinary perspectives, working together over a decade or more. Furthermore, the scientific enterprise is not limited to research, but also includes education of new scientists, and interaction with industry and with society at large to ensure that the results of the research get translated into socially useful products and services.

The basic organizational structure of NSF is not well suited to supporting larger efforts of this sort. A program officer for a particular discipline, with a limited budget and many more good proposals than the budget can support, is going to be reluctant to devote a major portion of the program's resources to a single activity, however worthwhile. Recognizing this limitation, NSF has established some programs designed to support activities on a larger and more interdisciplinary scale than individual disciplinary programs are likely to fund. Some target specific fields, such as engineering research or materials science. One general program that is available to all fields of science is the Science and Technology Centers program, or STC.

NSF subtitles the STC program "Integrative Partnerships," to indicate what it expects from them. A Science and Technology Center is based in an academic institution, but operates in coordinated partnership with a number of other organizations, including industrial firms, other academic institutions (including ones in other countries), public schools, private research labs, and so forth, as appropriate to the aims of the STC.

The names of some of the existing STCs give an idea of the kinds of topics they cover. NSF funds STCs for Behavioral Neuroscience, for Nanobiotechnology, for Integrated Space Weather Modeling, for Adaptive Optics, and for Environmentally Responsible Solvents and Processes, among others. Twenty-three STCs established in the late 1980s and early 1990s have now "graduated" from NSF support, but most of those are still actively at work with funding from other sources.

By NSF standards, STCs constitute a major investment. They receive funding at a rate somewhere between $1.5 million and $4 million per year, for up to ten years. The standards that applicants must meet to win funding for one are correspondingly high, as are the expectations for performance. Competitions for new STCs, which occur every two or three years, are lengthy affairs, requiring a statement of intent, followed by a competitive preproposal, followed by a full proposal from those who are invited to submit one after the preproposal competition, followed by site visits to those applicants whose full proposals fare the best under review, followed by awards to five or six institutions to establish new STCs. Once an STC is established, NSF participates more actively in its management than it does for regular grants, and reviews its performance carefully in deciding whether to continue funding it.

Applying for an STC is thus a major undertaking for an institution, usually led by a senior faculty member with a strong national reputation, but necessarily involving many other people at all levels on the faculty and in the administration. Anyone who considers submitting an STC proposal should without fail make early contact with the NSF program officers responsible for the STC program, for guidance on the timetable for the next competition, the procedures for applying, and whether the concept being proposed is likely to be competitive enough to be worth the effort.

Integrative Graduate Education and Research Traineeship (IGERT). The IGERT program is in a sense a counterpart to the CAREER program, extended from the individual level to the institutional level. Like CAREER, IGERT has the goal of more closely integrating teaching and research in science education. IGERT focuses on graduate education programs that lead to the doctoral degree. Through IGERT, NSF makes grants that enable institutions to establish new graduate programs with certain distinctive characteristics: they are interdisciplinary, they are innovative, and they successfully integrate teaching and research to a greater degree than traditional graduate programs.

There is an IGERT competition every year, making about twenty new grants. The grants are sizable, exceeding half a million dollars annually for five years, most of which goes directly to the support of graduate students enrolled in the supported program. The competition starts with submission of a preproposal. After a competitive review of the preproposals by specially constituted review panels, NSF invites some of the institutions to submit full proposals. Review of the full proposals leads to selection of the awardees. IGERT has its own budget, so IGERT proposals are only in competition with each other and not with the regular proposals submitted to NSF.

As for STC, application to the IGERT program involves a substantial commitment by the institution, first of time and effort devoted to the application process, and then of institutional resources to help sustain the new graduate education program if the application is successful.

Major Research Instrumentation (MRI). Regular program grants often include funds for the purchase of special research equipment, to meet the needs of the individual projects they support. Some kinds of scientific research, however, require equipment that is so expensive that it is difficult for a disciplinary NSF program to afford it within its basic budget. To help satisfy the need for very costly equipment in some research areas, NSF has established a separate annual competition for proposals for Major Research Instrumentation (MRI), which currently grants over $75 million per year for that purpose.

Through the MRI program, institutions can request grants for special-purpose research equipment costing from $100,000 to $2 million (slightly smaller requests are allowed in some fields of science, and from non-Ph.D.-granting institutions). The funds can be used to acquire existing scientific instruments or to develop new ones. Generally equipment funded through an MRI grant will be useful to a number of different researchers and different projects, and an MRI proposal is more likely to be successful if it demonstrates the breadth of use to be made of the requested equipment. Also, NSF expects institutions to integrate the instruments into their science education and research training activities, and the proposal should demonstrate how they will do this.

Initiatives in Special Topic Areas

The organizational structure of NSF follows disciplinary lines, as we mentioned earlier. Each year's new appropriation of funds to the NSF by the Congress flows down through this structure to set an annual budget for each of the many disciplinary programs that are part of the permanent structure. The budgets of the permanent programs don't vary a great deal over time; they may increase by a few percentage points from one year to the next to reflect general increases in the cost of doing research, but rarely increase substantially enough to enable a program to underwrite a whole new area of research without reducing its commitments to the ongoing areas it has been supporting.

This continuity has its advantages: it ensures a stable base of support to an active, productive field of research, and gives investigators a fairly good sense of the chances of being funded and of a realistic figure for a project budget. In a dynamic, ever-changing world like scientific research, however, it also has the obvious disadvantage of making it more difficult for NSF to respond quickly and effectively to the emergence of important new research opportunities – newly researchable questions at the boundaries between disciplines, for example, or new equipment or techniques that make possible whole new lines of inquiry. Also, science operates in a social context, and as new social issues and problems command public attention, they frequently have a scientific aspect, and the society expects its scientists who receive public support to help contribute to understanding and solving the matters.

To accommodate emergent needs and opportunities that are broader in scope and scale than the regular program structure can deal with effectively, NSF has come to rely on the mechanism of special initiatives. An NSF initiative is a commitment by the agency to devote extra funds and attention to some special topic or field of research, usually broad enough to cover the interests of two or more NSF Directorates, for a limited period of time, usually a few years. Initiatives don't normally acquire a permanent place in the organizational structure, but are managed by committees of program officers who run their own disciplinary programs as well.

Initiatives come and go over time, as the agency determines the need for new ones or decides to phase out older ones. We will mention a few here that are current at the time of writing, to show what sort of animals they are, but bear in mind that the list is likely to be different by the time you are reading this, and to continue to change.

- Information Technology Research (ITR) is a large, well-funded initiative to enable NSF to support a wide variety of research projects on information technology in the broad sense, beyond what the Computer and Information Science and Engineering Directorate (CISE) is able to do with its own resources. Because the advances in information technology touch on so many different areas of science, most of NSF participates in ITR, in contributing to its funding and in helping to manage the ITR competitions.
- Environmental Research and Education (ERE) is actually a collection of several different initiatives relating to the environment, including Biocomplexity in the Environment, Global Change Research, Long Term Ecological Research, and others. Again, NSF has an organizational unit devoted to the area, the Division of Environmental Biology, (DEB), but the initiative involves other NSF

units as well and supports multidisciplinary activities that go beyond what DEB would be able to support on its own.

- NSF participates as one of a number of government agencies in the National Nanotechnology Initiative (NNI), devoted to research on phenomena at the nanometer scale and to development of devices that operate at that scale. NSF runs its own special grant competitions in nanotechnology, managed by a group of program officers representing a broad spectrum of scientific disciplines.
- The Digital Libraries Initiative (DLI) also involves a number of government agencies, with NSF and other agencies running their own programs to support the establishment of new major information resources, based on the Internet, in a variety of fields in the sciences and humanities.

Each initiative has its own Program Announcement, or often a series of them for different funding competitions, its own deadlines, its own review procedures, and its own special criteria for evaluation of proposals. Part of the basic background preparation for anyone who plans to seek research funding, from the NSF or other agencies, is to study their Web sites carefully to find out what initiatives are currently active and whether any of them are relevant to the research to be done. You can also ask a program officer for advice, but you should know that program officers are not always fully aware of the full range of initiatives that are current or forthcoming, unless they have been directly involved in their planning or management.

Optional Mechanisms that Program Officers Can Use

The regular grant is the stock in trade of the program officer responsible for a disciplinary program at NSF. The program officer's job, however, is larger than simply managing the flow of proposals; the program officer is responsible for the health and growth of his or her field, and sometimes the regular grant isn't the best tool for the job. An NSF program officer has several mechanisms available to meet special needs. Program officers usually don't set aside funds in advance for these special purposes, but wait to see what requests come in, and evaluate them in the context of all the other ways they might use their program budgets to advance their fields.

Small Grants for Exploratory Research (SGER). An investigator
may call the program officer and describe a brilliant new idea, one
that could have great impact if it proves out, but requires some preliminary research before a full proposal can be prepared. Maybe it's a
risky idea, with a chance of failure that's too high for the tastes of most
reviewers, but with a potential for a really big payoff if it works. Or an
unpredictable and short-lived event may occur – such as a volcanic
eruption, a major flood, or a political coup – that warrants scientific
observation but may be over by the time the regular proposal submission and review processes could take place. To deal with situations
like these, the program officer has the discretion to make a limited
number of grants under the rubric of Small Grants for Exploratory
Research – SGER, or "sugar" grants as they are affectionately known
inside NSF.

SGER grants are for short durations, usually a year or less, and
for limited amounts, usually less than the average grant amount a
program awards. The program officer can put through an SGER grant
action on his or her own initiative, without external review, on a very
quick turnaround basis if necessary. The SGER process requires a
short proposal, but this almost always comes after the program officer
and the PI have discussed the matter thoroughly, and the program
officer has invited the PI to submit the SGER proposal. You should
never submit an SGER proposal without talking to a program officer
first and securing an invitation to do so; one that comes in out of
the blue, without prior consultation, will almost certainly be dead on
arrival.

Conference Grants. In some fields, conferences and workshops are a
vital part of the ongoing life of the field. Program officers can support
these from program funds if they feel the event is one that could
have a noticeable positive impact. A PI who wants to organize a
conference (or a workshop or a symposium; from here on we'll use the
word "conference" to cover all of these) submits a regular proposal
to the program, modified appropriately for the purpose (the NSF
Grant Proposal Guide has a section describing the special properties
of conference proposals). The program officer may choose to review
the proposal along with the regular research proposals or may use
special review procedures.

Here is some advice about conference proposals from a former NSF program officer who used to review (and fund) a lot of them. First, what makes a conference proposal competitive, a good candidate for funding? The key considerations are uniqueness of the concept and breadth of the impact. A uniquely conceived conference is one that brings together people who should be talking to one another for mutual benefit to their work, but for whatever reason are not doing so. It focuses on a well-defined specific topic, to ensure that the participants engage one another in productive discussion. A "class reunion" type of conference proposal, to bring together a set of researchers who are already in regular contact and collaboration with one another, is unlikely to generate much excitement; nor is a proposal for a conference with the tenor of a regular meeting of a professional society, in which participants present prepared papers on whatever they happen to be working on at the time, with no clear common theme. By and large, NSF programs are unlikely to fund the current edition of an annual conference; one-shot events are much better candidates for support.

A conference should also have broad impact, meaning that its results and its benefits should extend beyond the participants. The participants in a well-conceived and well-organized conference are likely to come away from the event feeling stimulated and inspired, with new ideas and approaches to try out in their own research. This is a valuable outcome, but may fall short of distinguishing the proposal as one to fund. The reviewers, and the program officer, want to see evidence that the conference will result in advances to the field among researchers who did not take part in the event itself. This normally means that the conference proposal should include a plan for publishing the proceedings, as a book or on the Internet. It also is a criterion for judging the conference topic, whether it is one that is of interest and significance to researchers beyond the immediate participants.

The conference proposal should be very specific in naming the prospective participants; a proposal that says "we will invite distinguished representatives from the different approaches to this question," without identifying them, has little chance of success. And it's a good idea to make sure that the participants know that they're named in the proposal. It is more than a little embarrassing to everyone concerned when a named participant learns during the review process that he or she is on the roster without having been consulted about it. The final invitations to participate, of course, will depend on the proposal being funded; everyone understands this.

The proposal should also include a specific agenda for the conference. This helps the reviewers judge whether it is well designed to meet its objectives – how much time there is for presentations, how much for discussion, how much free time, and in what order. And it is also helpful to reviewers if the proposal mentions other conferences that have been held on the same or a related topic, and how the proposed event differs from them.

People organizing conferences sometimes feel that the event will be more productive if it is closed to everyone but the participants. Although there may be some logic to this view, it nonetheless does not sell very well with reviewers and program officers. The funds distributed by NSF and other government agencies are public funds, ultimately derived from the nation's taxpayers. A conference supported from public funds should in principle be open to any member of the public who is interested enough to attend, unless there is a compelling reason to close it. This does not mean that anyone who wishes to must be allowed to speak – the organizer and participants control the agenda. Nor does it mean that the conference must occur in a large auditorium, when an ordinary classroom would suffice. It simply means that subject to reasonable limitations on available space, someone who wishes to attend all or part of the conference as a silent observer should be allowed to do so. In practice, the nonparticipant attendees are likely to be grad students at the host institution and faculty from the host or nearby institutions with an interest in the conference topic.

The conference budget will normally include travel and accommodation expenses for the out-of-town participants; rental costs for the meeting space and necessary equipment, such as audiovisual equipment; the costs of some modest refreshments for participants during the event; and the costs of preparing the proceedings for publication afterwards. NSF rules allow the payment of honoraria to participants, but it is generally a bad idea to include a request for honoraria in a conference proposal. If the conference is interesting enough to warrant support with NSF funds, it should be interesting enough to motivate participants to attend without financial inducement, beyond having their expenses covered. Likewise, the organizer is best advised to forego requesting salary support, even though the rules allow it. There can be some support for staff time to help organize the conference and prepare the proceedings for publication.

The lead time needed for seeking NSF funding for a conference can sometimes catch people by surprise. You really need to submit a conference proposal about a year prior to the event. It's going to take NSF about six months to review the proposal and decide whether to fund it. After you learn that you're going to receive the funding you requested, you need time to make all the arrangements, and the participants need time to prepare their own contributions when it's definite that the event will take place. These activities are likely to add another six months.

It often works well to plan a conference as a satellite event to some larger professional gathering, such as an annual national or international meeting, or a summer institute. Some of your preferred participants may be planning to attend the larger event anyway, and it can serve as an added enticement to others. Also, if you do seek an audience broader than just the invited participants, that's a good way to get one. If you decide to do this, you should coordinate it with the organizers of the main event. You'll be better off collaborating with them rather than conflicting and competing for resources, and chances are they'll be happy to publicize your conference in the meeting materials distributed to the attendees at the larger gathering.

Doctoral Dissertation Research Grants. Supporting graduate education in the sciences is a long-standing priority for NSF. The support comes in both more and less direct ways. There is an annual national competition for NSF Graduate Fellowships, awarded directly to promising students just entering graduate study. Most regular NSF grants include funds to hire one or more research assistants, who are graduate students in an area related to the topic of the grant project. Programs like IGERT and STC, mentioned above, provide significant additional support for graduate students. And some NSF disciplinary programs and divisions entertain and fund proposals to support the research projects that graduate students undertake for their doctoral dissertations.

Dissertation grants pay research costs that go beyond what the student or the institution would normally expect to pay for from their own resources – travel to a field site, for example, or a special piece of equipment, or fees for experimental subjects. They aren't fellowships; that is, they don't pay tuition, or stipends, or basic living costs, for which the student is expected to find other sources. Rather, their purpose is to enable students to undertake some valuable dissertation research projects that would otherwise be financially infeasible.

Applying for a dissertation grant is much like applying for a regular grant, by submitting a formal proposal, and the guidance on proposal writing in Chapter 5 is pertinent to proposals for dissertation research as well. Dissertation research proposals do have some special characteristics, though. The programs that offer them usually limit the maximum grant to a comparatively small amount, on the order of $12,000. Grants are usually for one year, rarely for more than two years, in keeping with the view that dissertation research projects should be completed within that sort of time frame. The proposals are shorter than those for regular grants, usually with a ten-page limit on the length of the project description. The grants do not include any indirect costs paid to the institution (we'll be discussing indirect costs in more detail in Chapter 5). The student's dissertation advisor serves as Principal Investigator, with the student named as Co-PI.

The NSF programs that offer dissertation grants are primarily in the social, behavioral, and biological sciences. Even among the programs that do offer the grants, there is considerable variation in how large a role they play in the program's activities. Some programs award only a few a year, while other programs devote a substantial portion of their annual budgets to supporting dissertation projects and run a whole separate competition for the dissertation grant proposals. You can find out from the NSF Web site or from a program officer whether a program in your area of science offers dissertation research grants, and when to submit proposals.

Special Funding Mechanisms at the NIH

The National Institutes of Health is a collection of semiautonomous Institutes, as we mentioned in the previous chapter. Each Institute can and does establish its own special funding programs, as it sees useful in its area of concern, and there are also some NIH-wide programs for special purposes.

The Institutes generate new funding opportunities to stimulate research on particular topics that have assumed increased importance for scientific or social reasons. These come in two general forms, Requests for Applications (RFAs) and Program Announcements (PAs). An RFA is a one-shot deal (it might be repeated, but there's no assurance of that), stating that the Institute has decided to commit a certain amount of funds during one particular year to supporting research on the topic, and setting a deadline for the receipt of applications. A PA expresses an Institute's intention to support research on a given topic over a more extended period, and invites researchers to submit applications by any of the Institute's regular deadlines.

To serve the special needs of particular groups of researchers, the Institutes incorporate into their own activities some NIH-wide funding mechanisms. The mechanisms NIH favors are supplements to existing NIH grants, which may be targeted to underrepresented minorities, people with disabilities, or people whose research careers have been interrupted by family responsibilities and who wish to reenter the scientific workforce. In the cases of minorities and the disabled, the support can go to anyone from a high school student to a faculty member with a doctorate; for the career reentrants, a doctoral degree is required. The idea of the supplements is to provide additional funding to an ongoing research project supported by NIH, to allow the PI to add a targeted individual to the research team, at a level suitable to that person's training and experience. By joining an existing project, the person can get hands-on research experience in a supportive and intellectually stimulating setting, which can provide both motivation and background to move into an independent research career.

NIH also offers a suite of Career Development Awards to support biomedical research scientists at various stages of their careers, from those just completing a post-doc to senior scientists. The applications for these awards, and the review criteria for evaluating the applications, focus more on the individual's accomplishments and promise than on the details of the research project planned, although the latter are included as well. The NIH Web site has a convenient "Career

Award Wizard" that you can use to determine which category of Career Award suits your own circumstances.

International collaboration is as vital in biomedical research as in other fields of science. One of the NIH organizational units, the Fogarty International Center, supports international research and training programs, research grants, and fellowships designed to encourage and enable U.S. scientists to work with their counterparts in other countries, particularly on health problems that disproportionately affect the poorer countries of the world.

NIH has an arsenal of dozens of "activity codes," designating different types of grants that Institutes and programs can use for particular purposes. One of those codes, "R01," is a specific term for what someone at NSF would imprecisely call a "regular grant," and the R01 grants represent the major portion of NIH research funding. If need be, however, an NIH program can award an R03, a small grant; an R13, a conference; an R21, an exploratory or developmental grant; and so on. If your work falls within the NIH purview and you want to seek NIH support for it, your immediate task is to study the NIH Web site carefully to glean as much general information as you can, and then to communicate with an appropriate NIH program officer to zero in on how best to proceed in your particular case.

A Parting Thought about Special Funding Mechanisms

Throughout this chapter we've noted that some of the special mechanisms have funds set aside for them, and others don't. In most cases, it's fair to generalize that the ones with earmarked funding are agency activities that work outside of the regular disciplinary program structure; the special mechanisms that program officers use within their programs generally don't have funds set aside for them in advance, although there are some exceptions in individual cases. By and large, program officers prefer not to partition their budgets before they see and evaluate the funding requests they receive. A program officer usually puts a high priority on maintaining a uniform level of excellence across all of the activities that the program supports, and setting aside a portion of the program's resources for a particular category of support in advance of seeing the competition can work against that goal.

Nonetheless, most program officers are committed to the aims that the special funding mechanisms promote, such as increasing the participation in research of scientists from underrepresented groups, educating the new generation of scientists, and enabling new researchers to get a strong start on their careers. That commitment leads them to attend carefully and sympathetically to funding requests that would promote one of these goals. In making the discretionary judgments that program officers must frequently make in deciding which of many worthy applications to recommend for funding, they will include these matters as serious factors in their consideration. It is therefore an excellent idea for an applicant to make sure that the program officer is aware of any characteristics of the investigators or the project that warrant special attention, especially if these don't appear in the proposal. Sometimes there is a simple mechanism, such as a checkbox on the cover page of the proposal form, for conveying this sort of information, and the applicant should be diligent about marking these appropriately, but even in these cases some redundancy doesn't hurt in ensuring that the message gets across. The proposal still has to meet the standard of quality necessary to receive funding, of course, but in the all-too-frequent situation where the program officer has many more high-quality proposals than the program's budget can support, and must make choices among them, the special extra factors can play an important role in the choice.

5

Writing a Proposal

All right. Now that you've selected your topic, planned your project, and identified your potential funding sources, it's time to sit down and actually write your proposal. In this chapter, we'll describe a way to approach the job that should make it easier and make the result more effective.

The model informing the discussion here will be a proposal to the NSF. Most of what we say will be at a level that is general enough to apply to proposals to other agencies as well, but those may have special features that we won't deal with here. It's important to get specific guidance from the agency you're applying to, from its Web site and from a program officer in your area, to supplement the help this book provides.

The Audience

The first question to consider when you set out to write anything, proposals included, is "who is the audience?" When you know who is in your audience, and how they think, and what they expect, you're in a position to communicate your message to them confidently and effectively.

The audience for a research proposal has up to three major components. These go by different names at different agencies, but at NSF they are known as ad hoc reviewers, advisory panels, and program officers. At least one program officer will always be involved; ad hoc reviewers, or panels, or both, may also participate, depending on the type of proposal and what part of the agency is reviewing it. Let's look at each of these members of the audience.

Ad hoc reviewers are specialists in the field of the proposed research. The program officer responsible for the proposal selects them specifically for the particular proposal under review (hence the term "ad hoc"), on the basis of their expertise and their ability to act as impartial judges. The ad hoc reviewers receive the proposal by mail or electronic transmission at their own locations, and prepare and return their reviews privately.

The *advisory panel* is a group of five to maybe twenty or more senior researchers whose collective expertise covers the spectrum of research areas represented in the proposals the panel reviews. A panel may be a standing body that meets periodically to review the proposals for an established program, or it may convene only once to serve a particular initiative or competition. In either case, the panel meets together, often but not always at the funding agency, and discusses a set of proposals as a committee. A summary of the panel's discussion, along with its rating of the proposal and its recommendation as to whether to fund the proposal, are an important component of the review materials for the proposal.

Panelists are recruited on the basis of their expertise, their stature in the field, their breadth of interest and accomplishment, and their reputation for fairness and collegiality. The agency also tries to ensure that the panel is balanced along such dimensions as gender, ethnicity, and geography. A member of a standing panel serves for a defined term, usually three or four years.

We have already met the *program officer* in earlier chapters. The program officer is an employee of the funding agency. Qualifications for the job include the highest academic degree in the person's field, plus a number of years of successful experience as an active researcher. The nature of the work demands a person with a genuine interest in the broadest reaches of the field, and someone who is comfortable and adept at administrative tasks. The program officer has to represent the agency to the field, and the field within the agency. Representing the agency means accepting the responsibility to ensure that the program's activities respect and reflect the agency's policies and priorities.

The Project Description

The three audience components play overlapping but different roles in evaluating the proposal. Each part of the audience focuses its attention on different aspects of the proposal. To delve further into this matter, we need to break the proposal down into its major components.

A formal proposal has a number of prescribed sections, and we will return later in the chapter to a practical discussion of how to go about preparing each of them. For present purposes, however, we will focus on the project description. The project description is the central narrative portion of the proposal, where you set out what the proposal is about, what the project is to do, and how, and why. This is the portion of the proposal that any reviewer must study the most carefully in order to come to an informed judgment about the quality and promise of the project. The project description needs to cover a number of topics, which we will now mention in the order in which they usually appear, and then revisit with the eyes of the audience.

The proposal first needs to establish the *conceptual foundations* of the project: the hypothesis or question driving the research, how it emerges from the current state of our knowledge, and how it motivates the research program to be proposed.

Next comes a *literature survey*, giving a concise but thorough summary of work on and related to, the topic at hand, including your own work. The literature survey outlines the various approaches to the topic, and shows how the proposed project relates to and differs from them.

If you have had an NSF grant within the past five years before submitting your proposal, the project description must include a section describing the *results of prior research*. This typically occupies the first few (up to five) pages of the project description, although you can incorporate it into the literature survey if it seems appropriate.

The *project design* is the centerpiece of the project description. Here you present the details of what you're actually going to do. The sort of details you present will vary, of course, according to the nature of the research, but include materials, subjects, sites, methods of data-gathering, controls, methods of analysis, and interpretation.

It's essential to describe the *significance* and *broader impacts* of the project. NSF has come to place more and more emphasis on this in recent years, and now has an explicit requirement that a proposal must describe the broader impacts of the project as an integral part of the proposal narrative, and in the project summary, or the proposal will be returned to the applicant without review. Significance in the narrowly scientific sense is how the project will advance scientific knowledge beyond the boundaries of the specific research topic. The "broader impacts" NSF envisions relate to how the project will contribute to the scientific enterprise generally, especially in the educational realm, and to society as a whole.

The project description needs to include a plan for *dissemination of the results* of the research. The results of the project have little value until others have access to them. Dissemination includes first of all publication in an appropriate choice of media, but also preservation and sharing of data, samples, physical collections, and so on.

Finally, it is not amiss to indicate the *qualifications of the investigator(s)* responsible for the work. Although the proposal will include biographical sketches (including abbreviated lists of publications) for the PI and other key members of the research team, and the reviewers may know you by reputation, it is still a good idea to show that you are prepared to undertake the specific project proposed, especially if it is particularly novel research or a new direction for your work.

What the Audience Wants

Ad Hoc Reviewers. The ad hoc reviewers are your closest professional peers among the reviewing audience. They are the people who can be expected to know as much as you do about your topic. They will be the primary reviewers of the technical content of the proposal, and the core of the project description is aimed at them. It should thus be at a level the reviewers will respect, with content and presentation equivalent to an article in a professional journal.

Specifically, ad hoc reviewers will scrutinize the adequacy of the following elements of the project description.

1. The *survey of the background literature* needs to persuade the reviewers that you have done your homework and that you are

thoroughly familiar with what has been done to date on your research problem. Your proposal, and your research for that matter,
are likely to succeed only if you position yourself properly in the
historical context. There's no value in doing research that's already
been done and reported in the literature, but you also need to avoid
proposing research that is premature, research with prerequisites that
have not yet been met. Recall our discussion in the first chapter, on
topic selection, of the "novel vs. grounded" dimension. The literature
survey is the part of the proposal where you demonstrate that you
are at the right point on that continuum.

The literature survey is especially important for new investigators
and first-time applicants. This is what you offer reviewers in lieu of a
track record, the information you give them to let them judge whether
you understand your research area thoroughly enough to be able to
contribute to it.

You can err by making the literature survey too short or too long.
If it's too short, it won't inspire confidence in your grasp of the area; if
it's too long, it uses up space that you need for describing your own
project, and risks boring the reviewer. Usually two to three pages
of carefully constructed text should be about the right length in a
fifteen-page project description.

2. Reviewers will study the *project design* section attentively to
learn exactly what you are proposing to do. The kinds of information
presented here, and the level of detail, will vary according to the type
of research you propose. The best model, again, is the journal article.
A journal article is retrospective, describing research that has already
been completed, whereas a proposal is prospective, describing research that is yet to take place, but the same kinds of information are
relevant in both. For example:

- rationale: the logic connecting the hypothesis or question motivat-
  ing the project to the specific research plans you are proposing
- selection of subjects and/or materials: the nature and number of
  the people or animals or plants or rocks or whatever elements of
  the natural world your research is focusing on, and how you will
  gain access to or use of them
- data-gathering methods: Is the research experimental or observational? What is the experimental design or the observational
  protocols? What are the controls? Or is this a theoretical project,

offering a new way of integrating and accounting for data that
have already been reported? What are those data, and where do
you find them?
* methods of analysis: the mathematical or statistical tools you will
  use to organize your data and make sense out of them
* interpretation: how different possible outcomes of the research will
  bear on the hypothesis under investigation

The appropriate level of detail will vary according to the project.
In general, you should state explicitly the choices you are making at
those points where other experts know that there are choices to be
made. They may criticize your choices or suggest alternatives, but
they will criticize the proposal more harshly if you don't appear to
be aware of the choices that must be made.

The degree of emphasis on the various aspects of the project design
will also vary according to the nature of the project. A proposal for
a theoretical project, for example, may devote primary attention to
the rationale and the interpretation; in a more empirical project, the
proposal will focus more on methods of data-gathering and analysis.
You need to follow the standards that pertain in your particular area of
research, as you have come to understand them through your training
and experience.

3. The ad hoc reviewers are well suited to evaluate your plans for
dissemination of the results of the research. They have a good idea of
the methods for reporting results that are most appropriate to the
nature of the research and to the research community interested in
it. There are many more options today than there used to be, including:

> journal articles,
> research monographs,
> CD-ROM,
> Web site,
> conference presentations,
> combinations of the above, plus other possibilities.

The proposal should make clear which of these you're planning
so that the reviewers can judge your plans and either endorse them
or suggest improvements.

4. The ad hoc reviewers are also likely to have the clearest idea of your *qualifications* to undertake the project you've proposed, and this is one of the key points the agency asks them to comment on. Because they are experts in your field of research, they keep up to date on who is doing what in the field, and they have their own opinions of the quality of the work that various people are doing. If you have been active in the field, as we urged in the first chapter – attending professional meetings, publishing in widely read journals, and taking part in the ongoing daily conversation in the field (which these days largely takes place on the Internet) – the chances are very high that they already are aware of your work. This is a Good Thing; receive a request to review your proposal, they are likely to have a more positive initial disposition toward it than toward a proposal from someone they've never heard of.

Of course, your proposal has to live up to the expectations your persona has engendered. If you are new in the field and have little or no track record of significant scientific accomplishments, your proposal has the burden of making your qualifications evident to its readers. A thorough, professional, and insightful treatment of the literature survey and the project design will help to ensure that it achieves this.

5. If the proposal includes a description of the *results of prior research*, the ad hoc reviewers will be the primary judges of the quality of those results and their impact on the field.

NSF explicitly asks ad hoc reviewers to comment on the *broader impacts* of the project as well, and they will do so, but this is typically of less concern to specialists in the research topic than the other aspects that we've listed.

The Advisory Panel. Many NSF programs employ standing advisory panels as an essential part of the review process. The advisory panel, or just "the panel" as it's commonly called, plays a different role in the process, one that is complementary to the ad hoc reviewers. All of the panelists are accomplished researchers with extensive expertise in their own specialties, but the number and range of proposals they review make it inevitable that for a fair number of the proposals, no one on the panel has the specific expertise in the research topic that an ad hoc reviewer would have. Also, unlike the ad hoc reviewers, the panel sees the entire group of proposals under review at one time, and can evaluate a proposal in the context of its competition. Third, the panel considers and evaluates a proposal collectively, as a committee, instead of the solo performance of an ad hoc reviewer, for whatever effect that may have.

Given its nature and its role in the review, the panel evaluating a proposal will tend to focus on other elements of the project description:

1. The clarity of the *conceptual foundations* of a project, or the lack of clarity, is often more apparent to someone who isn't a direct expert in the proposed field of research. Experts tend to "read between the lines" and assume that they understand what someone is trying to say, when the actual verbiage reflects confusion on the PI's part. A panelist who has some relevant general expertise but is not absorbed in the specific subfield of the proposal is more likely to pick up on that confusion, or conversely to admire and appreciate a lucid presentation.

Sometimes, of course, a panelist *is* an expert on the topic of a proposal. When that happens, the panel discussion of the proposal can get very interesting, as other panelists cross-examine the expert to be sure that they understand the conceptual foundations of the project.

A good way to check on the clarity of the conceptual foundations presented in your proposal is to show a draft of the project description to colleagues who are generally knowledgeable but not specialists in the topic, and find out how well they understand it.

2. One of the panel's key contributions to the review process is to evaluate the *significance* of the proposed project. Ad hoc reviewers, as specialists in the research area, can generally be expected to enthuse about the significance of a project (or else to reject it utterly, which is also suspect). Panelists are less likely to take the significance of a proposed program of work as given or obvious, and more likely to form a judgment of the potential significance of the work to a broader community of researchers, beyond the specialists. A good proposal will help them to make this judgment favorably by pointing out the significance explicitly and clearly.

Again, if a panelist is a specialist in the topic, the other panelists may bore in on the expert during the discussion of the proposal, to satisfy themselves that the project is significant to others besides the specialists.

NSF also expects the panel to evaluate the *broader impacts* of the project, which as we described earlier means its contributions to science more generally, especially science education, and to the larger social good. Because of the breadth of perspectives the panelists represent, the panel may be better suited to this than the ad hoc reviewers.

Special Panels. The panels that we have been discussing in the preceding section are the standing panels appointed by many permanent NSF disciplinary programs to advise them in the review of proposals and other matters affecting the program. Review panels can also be appointed on a one-shot basis to evaluate the proposals submitted to a special competition of the sort discussed in Chapter 4. A special panel like this is a hybrid of advisory panel and ad hoc reviewers. The agency often waits until it knows the topics of the proposals that are coming in before selecting a panel of experts in those topics. The specific expertise that the panel can bring to bear in reviewing the proposals is thus more akin to what a regular program expects to get from its ad hoc reviewers, and the program officers managing the special competition can rely on the panel to evaluate all of the major components of the project description outlined above. But it is still a panel in the sense that it sees all of the proposals and evaluates them in comparison to one another, and in the sense that it reaches its conclusions by committee consensus rather than as an individual opinion.

The Program Officer. Every proposal review will involve at least one program officer. The program officer is the professional the funding agency hires to ensure that proposals receive a thorough, competent, and fair review. The exact role of the program officer varies from agency to agency, as we saw in Chapter 3, but is always significant. At NSF, program officers not only manage the review, but also make the final substantive judgments as to which proposals the agency will fund. Their recommendations are subject to review by division directors and grants officers (administrators who actually sign off on the funding commitment), but are rarely ever reversed on substantive grounds.

For regular proposals that request funding for one or two investigators for a project running two or three years, and submitted to one of NSF's disciplinary programs, a single program officer usually has full responsibility. In the special competitions, especially for the larger grants (described in Chapter 4), a committee of program officers usually take charge of a set of proposals in their general area.

Program officers have had some firsthand experience in research – it's a qualification for the job. Usually (although not always) the experience is in some subfield of the general area their program handles. But every program officer is responsible for managing proposals and projects in areas that far exceed his or her primary expertise. Therefore program officers rely crucially on ad hoc reviewers and panels for evaluation of the technical content of a proposal, as the primary input to the final process of deciding which proposals to fund. However, the program officer has a broader set of matters to consider as well in making these decisions, which we will examine in this section.

The program officer's judgment can't be arbitrary or capricious, of course. If a program officer recommends funding a proposal that didn't do as well in review as some other proposal that isn't being funded, he or she has to provide clear and persuasive justification for the choice. It is not at all rare for this to happen; indeed, the agency encourages program officers to exercise their best independent professional judgment to identify promising proposals that for one reason or another the regular review process may not distinguish. The agency does insist, however, that program officers be accountable for such decisions by documenting the reasons for them thoroughly.

The biggest constraint on the program officer's funding decisions is money. The review process usually serves up a far larger number of strong, fundable proposals than the program's budget can support. A key part of the program officer's job is thus to make priority choices among deserving projects. In making such choices, the program officer gives primary weight to the relative intellectual merit of the proposals, as established in the review, but must also consider other factors that relate to more general considerations – factors that fall under the rubric of "broader impacts" mentioned above. It is worth discussing those auxiliary factors in some detail, to add to your understanding of what your audience is looking for. If any of them pertain to your case, you should be sure that your proposal makes that clear.

The program officer may give special consideration to any of the following factors.

- The proposal is for renewed support of a project that the agency has been supporting previously. Program officers understand the value of continuity of support for sustained scientific investigations that extend past the lifetime of a single grant. Renewed support is never guaranteed, because the vitality of the nation's scientific enterprise demands that the available resources support the very best work, and periodic competition with new applicants for the resources is the best way to assure that a project remains a leading contributor. But when the program officer is faced with a situation in which several proposals are of roughly equal quality and the program can't fund all of them, the program officer may prefer to continue supporting a productive project instead of shifting the funding to some new project.

    A renewal proposal will include a section describing the results of the previously supported research, and the program officer will pay careful attention to these, and to the reviewers' comments about them, in deciding whether the project warrants continued funding. We will discuss renewal proposals further below.

- The proposal is in an area of research where the program doesn't support many other projects. A program officer is not just responsible for managing the review of the proposals that come in and the grants that result from the proposals, but also has the charge to help maintain the health and support the productive growth of an entire field of science, to the extent that the program's resources allow. One matter that concerns program officers is to maintain what they call "portfolio balance," where the "portfolio" is the full set of projects the program is currently supporting. The fields that the programs serve typically comprise a number of specialized subfields, and the program's responsibilities extend to all of them. If the program's portfolio is light in its representation of a particular area within the field, then a strong new proposal in that area is likely to get funding in preference to a proposal of equivalent

quality in an area where the program is already supporting many
projects.

You can go to the program's pages on the NSF Web site to see
a list of its currently active awards, and get a sense of whether
the project you're proposing is in an area that is lightly or heavily
represented on the list.

- The PI is a new investigator, who has only recently completed
training and become a full-fledged member of the research community. For any field of research to grow and prosper, it needs a
steady infusion of new talent and energy from young people joining its ranks of researchers. The program officer will be alert to
proposals from new investigators that fare well enough in review
to be in the fundable category, and may select some of these for
funding ahead of other proposals of equal merit from more established researchers. Again, there are special programs that target
young investigators, such as NSF's CAREER program, but they
don't meet the entire need, and program officers will try to ensure
that some of the funds in the regular competition go to support
the best new arrivals in the field.

- The proposal is from a primarily undergraduate institution, or
from an institution that doesn't often receive federal funding for
scientific research. Most of the research funds, from NSF and the
other funding agencies, go to the major research universities, understandably, because that's where the majority of researchers
work. NSF is keenly aware, however, that high-quality undergraduate institutions in the United States graduate a large number of
students who go on to graduate school and distinguished careers
in science, and is eager to support faculty at those institutions who
are carrying out strong programs of research that the undergraduate students can participate in actively.

NSF has established a formal rubric, Research at Undergraduate
Institutions (RUI), under which such proposals can be submitted.
There is no special RUI competition or set-aside funds; RUI proposals compete with regular proposals in the regular NSF disciplinary
programs. Two special features of RUI proposals, however, can be
advantageous for the PI. First, they can include an extra section not
allowed in regular proposals, called an "RUI Impact Statement,"

which allows the PI up to five additional pages to make a case for the positive impact a grant would have on the institution, particularly on the science education of undergraduate students there. Second, special instructions go to reviewers of RUI proposals, urging them to give special attention to the RUI impact statement in their evaluation of the proposal, and reminding them of the different characteristics of the research environment at undergraduate institutions, such as higher teaching loads and lack of graduate student research assistants, that may have had an impact on the PI's track record.

Even if a proposal comes without the formal RUI apparatus, the program officer is likely to notice that it is from an undergraduate institution, or from an institution that infrequently receives NSF support, and to give it some additional weight in the final decisions about which among the well-reviewed proposals to fund.

- The PI belongs to a group that is underrepresented in the research community, such as ethnic minorities, women, or the disabled. As we saw in Chapter 4, there are some special programs specifically targeted to such groups. The long-term goal, however, is to increase the group's representation and participation in the community to the same level as the more dominant groups and thus eliminate the need for special programs. People from these groups should share proportionately in the agency's regular funding of research. Program officers may therefore give extra consideration to a proposal whose PI is from an underrepresented group, in deciding which among a set of proposals of roughly equal merit will receive support.

- The proposal is from an institution in a state where federal money to support scientific research is seen less frequently than in some other states. The NSF and the other federal agencies that fund research are parts of the U.S. Government, and receive the funds that they disburse from appropriations enacted by the U.S. Congress. The Congress consists of representatives from all the states, and every representative and senator is understandably concerned to make sure that the people of his or her state share equitably in the government's largesse. As it happens, the nation's scientific establishment is not equally distributed among the states. The major research institutions tend to cluster in a few geographical areas across the continent. In Fiscal Year 2000, nearly one-third of the NSF funds spent for science and engineering research went to institutions in just three states – California, New York, and Massachusetts. This is not because NSF or its program officers had any special affinity for those states, it's simply because that's where most of the best-reviewed proposals came from. Nonetheless, congresspeople from other states where the share of NSF funding is much lower tend to notice and worry about such statistics, and to share their concerns with NSF officials who visit the Congress in search of further appropriations.

In response, the NSF has done two things. It has encouraged program officers to be attentive to good proposals from the less frequently funded states, and give them extra consideration in the final funding decisions, which is why we mention it here. It has also established a formal program called the Experimental Program to Stimulate Competitive Research (EPSCoR). EPSCoR has identified twenty-two states, plus Puerto Rico and the Virgin Islands, which have received less than a specified threshold percentage of NSF funding, and has established partnerships with them to cooperate with local leaders in developing programs that will help improve the science and technology infrastructure and increase the ability of institutions and individual researchers in those places to compete successfully for NSF support.

EPSCoR has its own budget, which it uses both directly, to make grants to the EPSCoR jurisdictions to further its goals, and also indirectly through co-funding proposals that come to regular NSF programs from institutions in an EPSCoR locale. The co-funding possibility is what interests us most here. This is not something a PI can apply for directly; it's an internal arrangement at NSF, whereby a program officer can identify a proposal that is (1) from an EPSCoR state and (2) competitive for funding, but not in the very top category of proposals that the program will fund with or without co-funding. The program officer can ask the EPSCoR office to supply a share of the funding for the project, if that would make it possible for the program to award a grant that it otherwise would not. But even though you can't apply for it directly, if you're eligible for this special consideration, you should call the program officer's attention to the fact. You can find a list of the eligible states on the EPSCoR pages of the NSF Web site.

For any of these factors that we've been discussing, there is little influence that you as a PI can exert on whether your proposal will benefit from them or not. You're a new investigator, or a member of an underrepresented group, or you're not. But you can make sure that the program officer knows about your status if it does fit one of the categories. The proposal includes some mechanisms, like checkboxes and special forms and prefixes on proposal titles, to enable you to convey the information, but you don't have to stop there. It doesn't hurt to communicate directly with the program officer, apart from the proposal, and courteously remind him or her of your status.

With all this discussion of special factors that may enter into the funding decision, it's important to remember that the program officer's most important consideration is the quality of the proposal, as determined in the review by ad hoc reviewers and/or panels. The other criteria are secondary; the program officer may consider them in the process of selecting among a set of proposals that are all of comparable, fundable quality, but will not fund an inferior proposal just to meet a policy goal. Some of the secondary considerations conflict with one another – you can't be a new investigator submitting a renewal proposal, for example. It's the program officer's job to balance all of the various considerations in putting together a selection of grant awards that collectively do the most to advance the field that the program represents.

Writing to the Audience

As we mentioned at the beginning of the chapter, the audience that will see a particular proposal depends on the kind of proposal it is and the part of the funding agency that is responsible for reviewing it. Some divisions in NSF, for example, use only ad hoc reviewers, some use only panels, and some use both. A program that regularly uses both ad hoc reviewers and panels may use only one of these mechanisms for reviewing certain types of proposals, such as doctoral dissertation research proposals. For some kinds of proposals the program officer may act alone, without other reviewers – SGER proposals are in this category, for example, and also some other kinds of small awards, such as international travel grants.

Fortunately, you can always find out what the review process will be and which types of reviewers the audience will include. The program announcement describing the regular disciplinary program or the special competition that your proposal is going to will include this information, and if it's hard to find there or you're not sure how it applies in your case, it's perfectly legitimate to ask a program officer to tell you how your proposal will be reviewed. You won't find out who the specific ad hoc reviewers will be because that's confidential (although you can and should offer some suggestions, as we'll describe later), but you can learn if there will be ad hoc reviewers.

If a panel is involved in the review, you may or may not be able to find out who is on it, depending on the agency and the program within the agency that you're dealing with. In recent years NSF has become reluctant to divulge the membership of its panels, although some programs post the information on their Web pages, and at some level of aggregation it is public information. NIH, on the other hand, posts the names of the members of its Study Sections or Scientific Review Groups and its Advisory Councils on its Web site before every meeting of those groups. This information is very useful if you can get it, because it makes the composition and perspective of the audience even clearer. If you're working with a program at NSF that will not name the members of its current panel, you may be able to get the names of former panelists. That's helpful too, as the type of people that NSF recruits for its panels tends to be fairly consistent. If you imagine yourself writing to a committee selected from the list of former panelists, you probably won't be too far off the mark.

Once you know who will comprise the audience for your proposal, you can let that knowledge inform your writing strategy. We've discussed at length how the different components of the audience approach a proposal they're evaluating. If you know that only ad hoc reviewers will be evaluating your proposal, your project description can emphasize the elements that particularly concern ad hoc reviewers; if only a panel is involved, you can adjust the emphasis accordingly. This is a subtle matter, and we don't want to make too much of it; the project description still needs to include all of the elements, presented in a professionally competent manner. But the length limits on a project description are tight, and must be respected, so you are not going to be able to write everything you know about every element of the project. You will have to make some priority choices about which parts of your narrative to flesh out more thoroughly and which parts you can treat more succinctly. Keeping the nature of your audience constantly in your mind gives excellent guidance in making those choices.

Brave New Cyberworld

You may have noticed that more of life takes place through electronic media than it used to. Research proposals are only partially an exception. The funding agencies vary in how thoroughly they have embraced the Internet as a means of doing business. Most of the ones we've discussed still expect to receive proposals on paper. The NSF, however, is different. The NSF has taken a strong leadership role in moving all of its interactions with the public onto the Internet, including the submission of proposals. Since October of 2000, NSF has required that all proposals come in electronically, unless the PI gets explicit permission to submit a paper proposal (which rarely ever happens).

The NSF's system for managing all of this is called FastLane.[2] Once you start to prepare a proposal for NSF, FastLane will become your intimate companion. Fortunately it works well, and the user interface is quite intuitive, so most people find it convenient to use. FastLane offers users extensive help, including a large online user's manual, and a help desk accessible by a toll-free phone call sixty hours a week. It also has a nifty playpen – a "demonstration site" where you can practice using all of the functions involved in preparing a proposal before you do it for real. You link to FastLane from the NSF home page, and then to any of the FastLane components from the main FastLane page. It's a good idea to explore the system a bit and read the "More About FastLane..." overview before starting to use it in earnest. Your Sponsored Projects Office has the primary local responsibility

---

[2] Why FastLane? No one will say for sure, but the system was conceived and first implemented when Dr. Neal Lane was the Director of the NSF. Draw your own conclusions.

for FastLane at your institution, and can often give you invaluable help in working with it.

Before you can actually begin to use FastLane to prepare your proposal, you have to be properly introduced. Your institution's SPO will do this for you. They will register you on FastLane as a PI, and will give you a password that you can use to gain access to the system for real use.

In the practical advice on proposal preparation that occupies the rest of this chapter, we will simply take working online in the Fast-Lane system for granted, as a fact of life. We will not give explicit instructions for using FastLane, because that would be redundant with the information you can get directly from FastLane itself, and in any case the procedures could well have changed by the time you're reading this. But the suggestions we offer for preparing the various components of the proposal will presuppose that you're working within the framework of the FastLane system.

The Other Components of the Proposal

The centerpiece of the proposal is the project description. That's where you address your audience directly, tell them what you intend to do and why, and try to persuade them of the merits of it. All of our discussion in the chapter up to this point has focused on the project description, and rightly so, because that's where you make your case for your project and that's what takes your most careful thought and attention.

A full proposal, however, has a number of other components as well, that you need to prepare properly. We'll turn our attention to those in this section.

Required reading before you begin actually to construct your formal proposal is the funding agency's official book of rules on how to do it. At NSF this is called the *Grant Proposal Guide*, or GPG; other agencies have various other names for their counterpart documents. Every federal agency that funds research has one, available online. You can link to the GPG directly from the NSF home page. The GPG lays out in detail the current official requirements that an NSF proposal must meet. We won't reiterate all the contents of the GPG here, but you need to become familiar with them and abide by them, or risk frustration and delay in your attempts to get your proposal submitted and reviewed.

The GPG specifies the formatting requirements for an NSF proposal, including the length limits on the various components. Applicants sometimes don't take these requirements and limits seriously, and that's a mistake, because they are strict, and strictly enforced. A proposal that exceeds the length limits by even a small amount will usually be returned unreviewed, and if that means you miss a deadline, too bad.

For most of the components of the proposal it won't be difficult to adhere to the length limits, once you know what they are, but for the project description it can be a real challenge. The length of the project description for most regular proposals is limited to fifteen pages (a few of the competitions for especially large grants allow more, and some of the special funding mechanisms described in the previous chapter allow fewer). Those fifteen pages have to include the charts, graphs, tables, and illustrations, as well as the text. Many PIs feel a desperate need for more space to make the compelling case they want to make for their projects, and some try to shoehorn in additional material by shrinking fonts and margins and adding appendices. To avoid these expedients, the GPG also sets minimum size requirements for fonts and margins, and rules out the use of appendices.

It's worth noting that these limits are not some arbitrary bureaucratic dictum. They are the price of maintaining the goodwill and continued service of the many scientists who review proposals for NSF, as ad hoc reviewers or panelists. Reviewing proposals is a burden for them, an interruption in their own research programs. They accept this burden because they understand its importance to the long-term good of the research community, but if it becomes too onerous they may not. NSF has found that the length limits are one effective way to keep the burden under control. And trying to evade the spirit of the limits while obeying the letter – by using small fonts, minimizing white space, and so forth – will cost you more in goodwill among the reviewers than the extra verbiage that you manage to add through these ploys will buy you.

While writing your project description and keeping within the length limit, it's important to keep a proper balance among the various elements. Don't get carried away with writing the literature survey, for example, and devote ten pages to that, leaving just five pages for describing the project design, the significance of the project, the PI's qualifications, and all the rest (believe me, it happens, there are proposals like that). The reviewers will take the space you allocate to each element of the project description as an index of its importance in your view, so you should be sure that you apportion the space according to how important each element is to the overall case you want to make. It may take two or three drafts and some editorial advice from friends and colleagues to get it right, but it's worth the time and effort.

If you are worried about being able to fit everything you want to tell your audience within the fifteen-page limit, take comfort in the knowledge that every proposal in the group being reviewed along with yours is meeting the same limit, and the grants will all go to proposals that are within the limit. You just need to allow yourself the extra time it takes to write a shorter proposal.

Cover Sheet

The proposal cover sheet may seem like its most routine, humdrum part, scarcely worth any thought. Some of it is, but there is an art to completing some parts of the cover sheet that warrants our attention.

Selecting the Program Announcement or the GPG. The first real choice you have to make on the cover sheet is to select the program announcement or solicitation the proposal is responding to. The most common choice here is the GPG, which covers regular proposals to regular disciplinary programs. Sometimes a different choice is called for, however. In the previous chapter we discussed a number of special funding mechanisms that the NSF has instituted for various purposes. Some of these – but not all – have special program announcements associated with them. CAREER, for example, and STC, and IGERT, have their own program announcements, whereas some of the alternative funding mechanisms that program officers may use within their own programs, such as SGER and conference grants, don't. You need to know before you submit a proposal whether there is a special program announcement for the category of grants that you're applying for. You can usually find this out from the NSF Web site; anything you come across in the list of "Crosscutting" programs will probably have its own separate program announcement, for starters, and other special activities you find at the directorate and division levels of NSF may also. When in doubt, check with a program officer. It's important to get this right, because if you don't, your proposal may float around in limbo at NSF until someone figures out where it's supposed to go, and you could miss a deadline as a result.

Selecting the NSF Organizational Unit. After you've selected a program announcement or the GPG, you then choose the organizational unit or units within NSF that you want to consider your proposal. Some special program announcements pertain only to a limited number of programs or divisions, perhaps just a single organizational unit, and you haven't much of a choice to make. If your selection is the GPG, however – which it's most likely to be – the full set of NSF divisions and programs is there for you to choose from. Then you need to decide how your work best fits into the NSF organizational structure. Sometimes this is simple and straightforward, but at other times it can be baffling, if you work in an interdisciplinary area that might pertain to any of several different NSF programs, perhaps in different divisions. Here is where you can really use the advice of a program officer; they're used to receiving and answering questions about the assignment of proposals to NSF programs for review.

Joint Review. FastLane lets you select more than one program to review your proposal. NSF often assigns a proposal to two or more programs for review, when its content falls within the range of activities supported by separate programs. You can signal that you think that is the way to handle your proposal by naming a couple of relevant programs on the cover page form. The responsible program officers will consider the proposal and decide whether it should in fact undergo joint review. If they agree to review the proposal jointly, one program will assume the primary role and take administrative responsibility for managing the review, and your interactions with NSF during the review process will be with that program. The reviewing programs don't have to be in the same division, or even in the same directorate.

When two programs review a proposal jointly, they normally both put it through their full regular review procedure, working independently of each other (although they will probably confer in the selection of ad hoc reviewers). At the conclusion of review by ad hoc reviewers and/or panels, the program officers get together to look at the results and to discuss how the proposal ranks for funding in their respective programs. If they both find the proposal a good candidate for funding, they start to consider the possibility of joint funding by the two programs, deciding together what an appropriate grant amount would be and how to share the cost between the programs.

There are pros and cons to joint review. A proposal going through joint review faces a kind of double jeopardy, but also a double opportunity. Ad hoc reviewers and panels representing different research communities with different perspectives and priorities will be evaluating the proposal, and it can well happen – and often does – that one program's review will come out much more favorable than the other's. This is an intrinsic, well-known problem for interdisciplinary research in other circumstances besides funding review, such as journal publications, presentations to professional meetings, and competition for institutional resources. Interdisciplinary work has to meet the quality standards of the different disciplines that it bridges in order to gain respect on both sides of the bridge.

The other side of the coin, however, is that interdisciplinary research which does in fact engender admiration across disciplinary borders has a distinct advantage in attracting attention and resources over work that is solidly based within a discipline. Scientists are generally aware that most of the exciting new discoveries – discoveries that will motivate whole new lines of research – are going to come from work that transcends disciplinary boundaries, and when they encounter a proposal for such work that is of high quality from the perspectives of each of the disciplines that contribute to it, they are likely to respond to it more enthusiastically than to other proposals of equal quality that don't bridge disciplines. Within the context of the funding agency, if two programs reviewing a proposal jointly both find it fundable, and are able to share the costs of funding it, that proposal is more likely to result in a grant award than a proposal of equal merit that one program must fund entirely out of its own budget.

Bear in mind that whether your proposal is reviewed by a single program or by two or more programs acting jointly, NSF makes the final decision about the assignment of the proposal for review. The NSF program officers understand the division of labor among NSF programs better than anyone outside the agency, and want to ensure that each proposal is assigned to the program or programs that can give it the most expert review. They will certainly take seriously the assignment selection that you request on your proposal's cover sheet, and will try to follow it, but they will make a different assignment if there is a strong reason to do so. If it's important to you to know the final review assignment of your proposal, you can check with a program officer about a month or so after you have submitted it.

Remainder of the Cover Sheet. There remain several pieces of information for you to enter on the cover sheet, and some of those deserve our attention here.

The first item is the proposal title. Creativity is normally a virtue, but not when giving a proposal a title. Choose the simplest, clearest, and most straightforward title that you can think of that aptly describes the research you're proposing. Avoid cute or humorous titles, titles containing puns or literary allusions, and titles heavy with jargon. Why? The title of the proposal will become the title of the project, if the proposal leads to a grant, and the titles of the projects that NSF funds are an important source of information about what NSF is doing. A wide variety of people scan the lists of titles of NSF-funded projects regularly – scientists keeping track of what's happening in their field, politicians who must decide on the budget appropriations to NSF, journalists seeking subject matter for articles, among others. These people are not looking for humor or style; they are looking for information, and they may give a project the kind of attention its authors would prefer to avoid if they have some reason to think it may be frivolous. An NSF program officer will usually change an inappropriate title before sending a proposal out for review, but you will do better to spare him or her that task.

The next items on the cover sheet form are the total budget request and the project duration and start date. You can ignore the budget total; that will appear automatically when you complete the proposal budget, which is in a separate FastLane module. You do need to enter the project duration and start date. We've already discussed the choice of project duration in some detail; all there is to add here is to note that you state the duration as a specific number of months, from six to sixty. The start date is the date that funds will become available if you receive a grant for the project. It can be on the 1st or the 15th of any month, in principle. In fact, you need to exercise some care and some thought in requesting a start date. The start date needs to be early enough to allow you to do the project you propose – if the project depends on your work during the first summer, for example, it won't be useful to have a project starting September 1. But at the same time, you need to allow enough time for the proposal to go through review and a grant action to be processed before you expect to start the project. NSF has a publicly stated goal of completing review and action on all proposals within six months, so if you allow for six months from the time you submit the proposal until your requested start date, you'll usually be all right. Start dates, like budgets and project durations, are negotiable; you can request the start date that you consider ideal, but it is possible that the program officer will come back to you after the review with the good news that your project will be funded, but the not-so-good news that you won't be able to start it until some later date than you had requested.

The next choice is identifying your Co-Principal Investigators, if any. Good research is frequently a collaborative endeavor, especially on topics that cross the boundaries of disciplines or specialties. Many projects will occupy two or more investigators, and it is appropriate to identify them as jointly responsible for the work. NSF requires, however, that a single individual serve as Principal Investigator, with collaborators acting as Co-PIs.[3] From NSF's point of view, designation as PI is not a matter of prestige; rather, NSF wants a single person as a point of contact for administrative matters relating to a proposal and to any grant that results from it, and as the person responsible for the conduct of the project and for reporting the results. Among the scientists working on the project, however, there may well be issues of prestige, authority, and career advancement involved in the selection

[3] FastLane allows you to identify up to four Co-Principal Investigators, besides the Principal Investigator. The numerical limit doesn't represent some philosophical position about the maximum number of cooks for the broth. It simply reflects the number of data fields that the NSF database allots for Co-PIs.

of one of them as PI, so this is something you will want to work out carefully and tactfully with your collaborators before you are ready to enter your proposal into FastLane.

You next need to indicate if your proposal is for renewal of a previously funded project, or if it is a preliminary proposal, or a full proposal associated with a preliminary proposal, or none of these. If you have current or recent NSF funding, and the new project you are proposing is a natural continuation of the work you were doing under the previous grant, then you should note that your proposal is a renewal proposal. As we mentioned earlier, this will sometimes give you an advantage in competing with other proposals of equal merit.

There are two types of renewal proposals at NSF, regular and accomplishment-based renewals (ABR). Most renewal proposals are regular, but you may opt for the ABR format. The difference between the two is basically in the allocation of space to the components of the proposal. The regular renewal proposal devotes the first few pages (up to five) of the project description to the results of the previously funded research, and then the balance of the fifteen pages to describing the new research to be done with the renewed funding that is requested. An ABR proposal gives a brief summary (no more than four pages) to describing the new work to be done, and attaches reprints and preprints of up to six publications resulting from the prior research. Both types of renewals have to include a section with information on human resource development activities associated with the previously funded project – naming graduate students who participated in the research; describing courses and seminars and training associated with the research, especially for undergraduates; and reporting any special accomplishments in the development of scientists and engineers from underrepresented groups.

Clearly you want to choose the renewal proposal format that will make the best case for your continued funding. If your previous project resulted in a prolific set of publications that are likely to impress the reviewers and the program officer, and lead them to want to help you keep up the good work, the ABR is the way to go. If the major publishable results of your project still lie ahead, however, a regular renewal proposal will serve your purposes better. One point to bear in mind: you can't have two successive ABR renewals. You should also be aware that ABR proposals are much more common in some programs than others, and it's a good idea to check with the program officer first before deciding to use the ABR format.

Some NSF competitions, primarily for larger grants, require a preliminary proposal or preproposal initial submission, followed by invitations to submit full proposals based on the review of the preproposals. The program announcements for these competitions spell out the requirements. If your proposal is a preproposal for one of those competitions, or a full proposal associated with a preproposal, you indicate that fact on the cover sheet.

The form next asks you to identify any other Federal agencies to which you have submitted, or will be submitting, the proposal or one that is substantially equivalent. It's important to the program officer to know this, so take care to make the appropriate entries. You can make up your own abbreviations, as long as they're clear and unambiguous. And specify the actual agency that you're submitting to, not some larger parent organization, for example, NIH rather than HHS, or ONR rather than DOD. If you think you may submit the proposal elsewhere but aren't sure yet, go ahead and make the entry; it's better here to err on the side of overinclusion.

Your Sponsored Projects Office will complete most of the rest of the cover page form for you – information about the awardee and performing organizations, various certifications. There is just one additional section that you need to attend to carefully, labeled "Other Information." This is a set of checkboxes, each with a reference to some passage in the GPG. You should exercise great care in deciding which, if any, of the boxes to check. Don't assume from the brief label on the box that you know what it means, but turn to the referenced section in the GPG and study it to see whether it pertains to your case. When in doubt, don't make an entry until you've checked with your SPO or an NSF program officer. Each box checked in this section triggers a special set of requirements and procedures at NSF and maybe at your institution as well. In some cases those procedures may not actually be necessary, based on the real contents of your proposal, but if you check the box they will have to happen anyway.

The checkboxes include ones that indicate that your research involves human subjects, or vertebrate animals. Research in these categories imposes certain special requirements on investigators and institutions, concerning both the proposal itself and the management of the project if the proposal leads to a grant, for the protection of the human or animal subjects. We will discuss these requirements in detail in Chapter 6, on research ethics and responsibilities.

References Cited

A good bibliography is an important part of the proposal. It helps reviewers get a better idea of your command of the subject, and enables them to track down references that support claims in the proposal that they may find surprising. The program officer may also make use of your bibliography to help identify reviewers for the proposal, because it will cite others who are working or have worked in the same research area. You should thus be thorough in compiling the bibliography, but also judicious (another Goldilocks choice). That is, you should avoid stuffing in everything under the sun that has ever been written on your general research topic, but keep the references focused and relevant to your proposal. It's a good idea to include references to papers and books by people that you know or believe will be among the pool of possible reviewers of your proposal, if they are in fact relevant to your work. It's even more important to have read and understood every publication you list in the bibliography; it's a major and potentially fatal embarrassment to a proposal if it makes an unqualified assertion that a reviewer knows is contradicted by one of the books or articles cited.

You can use the same format for references that you would use in a journal article. Be sure to have a reference for every citation in the text of the project description; failure to do this is a sign of sloppiness. The "References Cited" section of the proposal is the only section that has no length limit, so make good use of it.

Biographical Sketches

The biographical sketch in an NSF proposal is an abbreviated *curriculum vitae* (CV). There should be one for the PI and one for each of the Co-PIs. The maximum length of a bio sketch is two pages, in which you need to include the same basic information about your education, your professional experience, honors and awards received, and so forth that you include in your regular CV, along with a limited list of publications. The list of publications is limited to no more than five that relate directly to the proposal, plus up to five more that you wish to list to remind reviewers of your research accomplishments. You must also provide in the bio sketch a list of your collaborators, concentrating on those you have collaborated with in the past four or five years, plus your dissertation advisor and any dissertation students you have advised. "Collaborator" means someone with whom you've co-authored a book or paper, or worked with seriously as a research partner; it does not include everyone you correspond with, or talk to at professional meetings. The purpose of this list is to help the program officer avoid asking someone to review your proposal who cannot do so because of a conflict of interest arising from their professional relationship with you.

FastLane allows you to save bio sketches to update and reuse in future proposals.

Budget

It's natural to worry a lot about the budget, because that's the direct statement of the money you're asking the funding agency to provide. If you've planned your project out carefully, however, the proposal budget is relatively easy to prepare. The important thing is to let the project plan drive the budget request. The first section of the budget, for example, is for project personnel. You should have already decided how many people in what categories (for example, PI, senior investigator, technician, graduate student, and undergraduate student) it will take to do the project you have in mind, and how much time will be required of each of them. Then all you have to do is fill in the relevant blanks on the budget form.

One highly relevant blank is the salary amount for each person working on the project, but that is something you don't have to decide. Your Sponsored Projects Office maintains a compendium of salary information for every type of job your institution has. For this and other information that they have to provide, it's essential to enlist your SPO to help you prepare your proposal budget. They're going to have to sign off on the proposal before it goes to the funding agency anyway, so it will save you time to get their cooperation in preparing it, especially the budget. Besides the salary information, the SPO also knows the formulas for fringe benefits and for indirect costs, which have to be included in the proposal budget and which you are unlikely to know, and they may well have wise advice to dispense about other budget items as well, based on their experience in submitting other proposals and administering grants.

After personnel, the next section of the budget form is for equipment. Not everything you might ordinarily consider equipment should be listed here, but only those items whose cost exceeds $5,000. Most computers and many other kinds of research equipment cost less than that, and they fall into the "materials and supplies" category on the budget. In many fields of science, few projects will require equipment of the kind that gets listed in this section of the budget.

Travel costs associated with the project have a budget category of their own, subdivided into domestic travel (including Canada and Mexico, as well as all of the United States) and foreign travel. Travel may be required for direct purposes of the research, to get to a field site, for example, or for visiting collaborators in other locations, or for going to professional meetings to present and discuss the results of your research. Often the program officer will allow a certain amount of money for travel without specific explanation or justification. We'll come back to these "rule-of-thumb" budget amounts in a moment.

The budget category labeled "Participant Support Costs" applies primarily to proposals for conferences and workshops, in which the purpose of the grant is to bring a number of people together for a limited period of time to accomplish some purpose. The participants receive travel and subsistence costs, and possibly stipends, and those costs appear on the budget in this section.

The final major budget category is the miscellaneous "Other Direct Costs," where you enter the amounts budgeted for materials and supplies, publication costs, consultant services, computer services, subcontracts, and other items not covered elsewhere. A number of rules and standards cover the details of what sorts of things these items do and don't include, and what costs are allowable. You can get an initial idea of such details from the GPG, and further guidance from your SPO and from a program officer.

Many program officers have a general notion of the basic resources it takes to carry out a normal research project in their field of science – how much time from the PI and other senior investigators, how many graduate students, how much travel, baseline budgets for materials and supplies and for publication costs, and so on. If a proposal is well enough reviewed to warrant awarding a grant to support the project, the program officer expects the grant to include at least those amounts, and possibly more, if the needs of the particular project require it. Here we'll call these "rule-of-thumb" budget norms. It doesn't hurt, and may help you in preparing your budget, to ask your program officer for his or her rules of thumb for analyzing proposal budgets. This information can give you valuable guidance in knowing how much justification you need to provide for your budget requests, and at what points in the budget. To the extent that your budget conforms to the rules of thumb for your field, you won't need to offer much, if any, justification for your requests. Where it exceeds the norms, you do need to give explicit and thorough explanations for the added costs in terms of the genuine requirements of your project.

The budgets for most proposals going to the NSF will add on at the end a substantial amount for "Indirect Costs." There's no decision for you to make here; the amount is determined by a formula, and your SPO will compute the correct amount for your proposal and add it to your budget. You may be curious, however, about the purpose of this substantial extra chunk of money that's tacked onto your budget, so it's worth a little explanation. The theory behind indirect costs is straightforward. The items listed in the various major categories of the budget – personnel, equipment, travel, materials and supplies, and so forth – are all direct costs of doing the research proposed, that is, they are the immediate resources required to carry out the project. They aren't the only costs, however. The institution provides space – office space, lab space, storage space – to do the research in, and pays to equip that space with furniture, light, heat, air conditioning, running water, bathrooms, and the other necessities of everyday living and working. It also provides necessary services like security, maintenance, cleaning, landscaping, communications, a library, a computer network, and administrative services. All of these things cost money, but it's not practical to try to figure out exactly how much of all these overhead costs a particular research project incurs. Instead, the government allows the institution to add up its total expenses for all its costs of this sort over the year, and to determine what percentage of its overall budget the overhead costs represent (that's oversimplified, but it's the basic idea). It can then add a comparable percentage to the direct costs of any grant it receives from the government.

NSF explicitly prohibits its program officers from encouraging PIs to negotiate reduced indirect cost rates with their institutions to make the overall cost of their projects more affordable within a program's budget.[4] Some PIs still manage to do this, and it may in some cases be helpful, but don't put your program officer on the spot by asking whether a reduced indirect cost rate would improve your proposal's competitive chances. Ironically, you may have a better chance of reducing the indirect cost rate at a smaller institution, one that receives few NSF grants and doesn't depend on them as a source of income, than at a major institution that has to be careful about setting precedents that could lead to diminishing their revenue from indirect cost reimbursements.

Another small item on the budget form that may arouse your curiosity refers to "Cost Sharing." NSF has a general requirement that institutions receiving NSF grants contribute to the costs of the supported projects. For regular grants, the cost-sharing is a small percentage of the total grant amount; for some special competitions, there may be a larger percentage required. The institution has a variety of ways to satisfy this requirement, none of which is likely to have any impact on you or your project one way or the other. Again, leave it to your SPO to complete this item correctly.

When you have finished filling out the budget form, FastLane will automatically compute the total and display it in the appropriate place on the cover sheet.

In general, it's to your advantage to keep your budget as lean as you can, up to a point. A tight, well-justified budget shows reviewers that you have thought your project through carefully. The program officer appreciates it, both because it means less work in figuring out what the budget really ought to be, and also because it will not take such a big bite out of the program's funds. Some PIs believe that the program officer is automatically going to reduce their budget by

---

[4] At NIH this isn't an issue, because NIH sets aside sufficient funds to pay all indirect costs on its grants before allocating budgets to programs. At NSF the indirect costs must come out of the program budget.

some arbitrary percentage, and so inflate the budget they submit to allow for that, but a program officer who makes arbitrary budget reductions is guilty of poor practice. The program officer's job is to determine as best as possible what it will really take to enable the project to happen, and to see to it that the grant covers the genuine needs. You should provide a budget that gives the program officer the information needed to make that determination.

There's no point, however, in submitting a budget that is obviously inadequate to the needs of the project you're proposing, in an attempt to improve your chances of being funded because your budget is so low. The reviewers will simply conclude that you don't understand the work you're doing well enough to come up with a realistic estimate of its cost. As we've said before, first plan your project carefully, and then let the project plan drive your budget, making your best and most honest guess as to what each component of the project will actually cost. Budgets are negotiable, and you may not get everything you ask for, but ask for what you believe you need.

Current and Pending Support

As we saw in Chapter 3, there may be several different possible sources of support for your research. In general, it's fine to apply to as many different funding agencies and organizations as will accept your proposal, and it's a good idea to do so. (There are some restrictions on this, particularly in the biological sciences, but they don't affect first-time applicants as a general rule.) What's important, however, is to make sure that everyone you apply to for funding has a full record of any current grants that you have, and of all of your proposals that are currently under consideration somewhere else, or that you plan to submit somewhere else in the near future. This includes grants from and proposals to private foundations as well as government agencies. The "Current and Pending Support" section of the proposal is where you give NSF this information.

For every current grant and pending proposal, you give the title of the project, the source of support, the total award amount granted or requested, the starting and ending dates of the grant or requested grant, and your time commitment to the project. The PI and each Co-PI must provide these data. It's important for the reviewers and the program officer to have a complete record here. The reviewers need to know in order to evaluate whether you will have the time you need to do the project you're proposing. The program officer has to ensure that the agency doesn't duplicate or overlap funding from some other source, and may also want to discuss the possibility of joint support of your project with other funders that are considering your proposal.

FastLane allows you to save the information you enter in the Current and Pending Support module for updating and use in other proposals.

Facilities, Equipment, and Other Resources

Some types of research require major equipment or special facilities to carry out. If your research is in this category, you need to provide NSF and the reviewers assurance that you have access to what you need in order to do what you propose (aside from the equipment that you are requesting in the proposal). This section of the proposal gives you space to list the specialized equipment and facilities available to you to do your research, at your institution or elsewhere. Don't bother to list relatively common, small, inexpensive items like computers, pH meters, or tape recorders that any reviewer would assume you have. What you need to report here are things like electron microscopes, mass spectrometers, magnetic resonance imaging machines, chimpanzee enclosures, and so on (but only if your research depends on them, of course). Try to anticipate what a reviewer is likely to wonder about – what you would wonder about if you were reviewing someone else's proposal for the same project – and provide the information that meets the need.

Supplementary Documents

The best general advice about this module is to ignore it completely. A few special competitions may require a particular supplementary document with the proposal; if so, the program announcement will make that clear. Or occasionally a program officer may ask you to provide some supplementary document. Unless you receive specific instructions to do so, don't add any supplementary material to your proposal. Doing so without instruction or permission constitutes a violation of the proposal length limits, and will probably result in your proposal being returned to you unreviewed.

Project Summary

Although the project summary appears at the beginning of the proposal, and it is the first thing reviewers will read, we have deliberately deferred it to near the end of the chapter, because you should write it last, after you have written the rest of the proposal. Once you have written and rewritten the project description and added the other components of the proposal, which may remind you of yet other things you should include in the project description, it will be easy to write a concise, informative summary. If you try to write the summary earlier, you will just end up having to rewrite it later, maybe several times.

One thing to keep in mind about the project summary is that it may end up with a much broader audience than the rest of the proposal. If your proposal results in a grant, the NSF will publish the summary (possibly edited) on its Web site, and *many* people will see it – other scientists in your field and related fields who want to keep up with the most recent work, students, journalists who want to pass on interesting new research to their readers, political types who want to see how the NSF is spending the taxpayers' money, and members of the general public just surfing the Web. As with any other writing, you want to keep your audience in mind. In writing the project summary, this means keeping it intelligible to an educated general audience, with a minimum of technical terminology.

NSF now requires that the project summary contain two distinct sections, the first describing the intellectual content of the project and the second its broader impacts, thus addressing the two primary review criteria. You can divide up the available space between the two sections as you see fit, but the whole summary should fit into a single printed page.

Begin the section on intellectual content with a one- or two-sentence statement of the principal aims of the project. Describe briefly the current state of our understanding of the topic to place the research in its scientific context, then summarize the main research activities. Write this as an abstract of the project that will be done if the grant is awarded, not as an abstract of the proposal – don't use phrases like "we propose to" or "if funded we will."

In the section on broader impacts, describe the scientific significance to your field and others of the results of the research; the potential for applications in technology or medicine or social services or environmental matters; and the educational impacts of the project on students at your institution and elsewhere. Keep your remarks descriptive rather than evaluative, that is, don't sound like you're praising or hyping the project, just describing it.

It's useful before writing your project summary to go to the NSF Web site, pick a program that interests you, follow the links in that program's Web pages to the list of grant awards that the program administers, and look at the abstracts (i.e., project summaries) for some of the awards. That will give you a feeling for the style and content standards that prevail in your field. The program officer has to edit project summaries if necessary before posting them on the Web site, so you'll be doing your program officer a favor by doing it right in the first place.

List of Suggested Reviewers

FastLane calls this form "optional," but it's an option you should certainly exercise. This is your one opportunity to have some input on how your proposal is reviewed, and you should absolutely take advantage of it. The program officer will appreciate your suggestions, because it will ease his or her task of identifying a set of reviewers for your proposal.

You can make both positive suggestions – people you would like to have review your proposal – and negative ones – people you do not want as reviewers. There are some considerations to bear in mind in both cases.

Your list of positive suggestions should name four to six possible reviewers. Generally the program officer will try to send the proposal to about six ad hoc reviewers, and will want to include a couple of your selections among the six. You need to name more than two, however, because some reviewers you suggest may not be possible choices, for reasons that you would have no way of knowing. They may already have been selected to review another proposal; they may have a proposal pending themselves; or they may have had a proposal of their own recently declined. Any of these factors might keep the program officer from asking them to review your proposal. If you name a few extra possibilities, that will improve the chances that some of them will be available as reviewers of your proposal.

On the other hand, if you name more than four to six possible reviewers, you may be doing yourself a disservice. The program officer may well want to use some reviewers besides the ones that you suggest. If you suggest a long list of reviewers, that may preclude the program officer from using some of the people on the list who might otherwise have been selected.

For each of the reviewers you suggest, provide their institutional affiliation and their e-mail address. That will enable the program officer to locate them and ask them to review the proposal, even if they are not currently in the NSF reviewer database, and to know which of several reviewers with the same name you are referring to.

You needn't hesitate to make negative suggestions as well. The program officer understands that all sorts of complex and conflicting interactions can take place between people working in the same field, and is glad to have the information and will honor your request if possible. You don't have to give any reason for your request, and indeed you probably should not. There are a couple of caveats to keep in mind, however. First, you have to name specific individuals, not categories of people. Don't ask the program officer to exclude all people following a particular theoretical paradigm, or all graduates of a certain university, from reviewing your proposal. Second, don't exclude so many people that you exhaust the pool of possible reviewers. In some highly specialized areas of research, there may be only a handful of people around the world with the expertise to review your proposal, and if you ask to have a number of them excluded, you may be making the program officer's task of finding knowledgeable reviewers impossible. In either of these cases the program officer will likely be unable to honor your request.

Only the program officer will see or know about your suggestions, positive or negative. Neither the panel nor the ad hoc reviewers need this information to evaluate your proposal, and indeed it might influence them in ways not related to the merits of your proposal, so the program officer will not tell them about it. That will help to assure that your suggestions will remain confidential, as they should.

Craftsmanship

For some reason, scientists often underestimate the importance of craftsmanship in proposal writing, perhaps on the premise that the significance of their proposal is in the content, and the form and presentation are incidental. It's certainly true that *what* you are going to do is the important thing. But when you describe your research plans to others who must evaluate them, you want their full attention on the substance, and every lapse in presentation is a serious distraction. Also, whether fairly or not, sloppiness in presentation inevitably raises the question in a reviewer's mind as to whether the PI may also tend to sloppiness in the laboratory.

It's therefore worth the extra time it takes to make sure that your proposal is free of typos, that there are references for all of the citations, that the axes on graphs are properly labeled, and so on. Ask a couple of colleagues to help you with the proofreading; fresh eyes will often spot errors that you have been systematically overlooking. Do all of this *before* you pass on the proposal to your SPO for final approval and submission to NSF. Once the proposal has been submitted, your opportunities to change it become severely restricted.

6

Research Ethics and Responsibilities

When you conceive of a research project, and design it, and propose it to a funding agency, you take on some obligations. As the intellectual progenitor of the project, you are accountable for its scientific soundness. You also have a broader set of ethical and administrative responsibilities, which we will explore in this chapter. They pertain to all stages of the project: writing a proposal, carrying out the research, and reporting on the results.

Scientists have always understood that they are subject to a set of ethical constraints and expectations. For a very long while, these were taken as implicit, an unwritten code of behavior that new people entering the field would absorb in informal ways, through their interactions with established professionals. A number of well-publicized cases of scientific misconduct in recent years, however, have suggested the need for a more explicit set of rules, with enforcement mechanisms. There is now a substantial and growing body of regulations governing the conduct of research. These are still a work-in-progress, evolving amid ongoing debate among scientists about the tradeoffs between freedom of inquiry and effective research, on the one hand, versus the need to ensure that the research does no harm, on the other. The principles that we will discuss in this chapter are basic enough that they are likely to survive, but the ways of interpreting and implementing them may evolve over time, and new ones may emerge. You should plan, therefore, to devote some time and effort to studying and understanding the documents that set out the standards of conduct that apply in your field of research. Funding agencies and professional societies are the best sources for the current versions of these documents.

Human Subjects

Arguably the most important ethical requirement of any scientist is to protect the well-being of the people who participate in a research project, whether as collaborators, students, or research subjects. The general body of laws and regulations promoting safety and privacy and prohibiting discrimination and harassment apply with equal force to researchers as they do to any employees in any workplace. People who serve as the subjects of research, however, are a special case, and require special protections. Not all sciences use human research subjects, but many do, especially in the biomedical, social, behavioral, and cognitive sciences.

After years of discussions among the research communities that deal with human subjects and the government agencies that support that research, a set of best practices was codified into a Federal regulation called the "Common Rule." The Common Rule (CR) establishes the fundamental U.S. Government policy on the protection of human subjects of research, and applies to all government agencies that sponsor research, internally or by external funding through grants or contracts. You can find a thorough and clear discussion of the CR, including the text of the regulation itself and answers to an extensive set of frequently asked questions about it, in the NSF Web site, by searching on "human subjects." Here, we will just touch on the highlights.

The basic principles underlying the CR are that human subjects of research should give informed consent to participate, and that participation in the research should not expose them to risks greater than those of ordinary life; or if there are risks, that the subjects should understand them, the researchers should attempt to mitigate the potential harm, and the potential benefits should equal or exceed the risks. There are special provisions for subjects who are presumably unable to give informed consent, such as children or the mentally ill.

The CR defines "human subjects" as living individuals about whom a researcher obtains data through intervention or interaction with the individual, or identifiable private information.

The CR establishes a mechanism for reviewing all proposed research projects and certifying that they comply with the requirements for protecting human subjects. An Institutional Review Board (IRB) at each research institution has this responsibility. The CR goes into some detail regarding the composition of the IRB; in brief, the members of the IRB must be experienced professionals who can exercise sound judgment about the treatment of human subjects from diverse scientific, legal, and social perspectives. No proposal involving human subjects can be funded by a government agency until the IRB has certified its approval.

The provisions of the CR were written primarily for biomedical research, but also apply to other types of research that employ human subjects. To avoid wasting the time of researchers and IRBs in reviewing proposals for projects that self-evidently pose little or no risk to subjects, the CR includes a set of exemptions from IRB review for particular types of research. The exemptions are for educational research; research studying data that have already been collected; research on public benefit or service programs; research on the taste, quality, and consumer acceptability of food; and most importantly for scientists who work with human subjects, "research involving the use of educational tests (cognitive, diagnostic, aptitude, achievement), survey procedures, interview procedures, or observation of public behavior." The latter exemption covers a great deal of social, behavioral, and cognitive science research.

The exemptions include a number of qualifications and exceptions. The exemption for tests, survey procedures, and so forth does not apply if the information obtained by the research is recorded in a way that allows the human subjects to be identified, directly or indirectly, *and* disclosure of the information could place the subjects at risk of criminal or civil liability or could damage their financial standing, employability, or reputation. If both of these circumstances are true, the IRB must review the research and certify that the project is designed in a way that will protect the interests of the subjects.

Besides the exemptions, there are a number of other categories of research that place human subjects at minimal risk, and are eligible for expedited IRB review. These change from time to time, as technology and research programs change, so rather than having to go through the cumbersome process of amending the CR, a Federal regulation, the NIH maintains a list of the currently eligible categories, accessible on its Web site. Eligible research includes collecting biometric data through noninvasive and nonhazardous procedures, audio and video recording, and research on individual or group characteristics or behavior not covered by the exemption just discussed, along with some other categories that pertain primarily to biomedical research. "Expedited" IRB review is faster and less stringent than full review; usually a single member of the IRB examines the proposal and certifies IRB approval.

Only the IRB can decide whether a particular proposal for research involving human subjects is exempt from review, or eligible for expedited review. Neither the PI, the department chair, nor the dean can make this determination. If your research project uses human subjects in any way, or if you think others might reasonably believe it does, you should check the "Human Subjects" box on the proposal cover sheet form, and have your local IRB pass judgment on whether your project is exempt from IRB review, eligible for expedited review, or requires full IRB review and approval. There are spaces on the cover sheet form for the IRB to declare the proposal exempt from review or to certify its approval.

Although the IRB must certify its approval of a proposal before a grant can be awarded, IRB approval is not normally required before the funding agency sends the proposal out for review. You can thus submit the proposal to the agency in time to meet the deadline or target date without having to wait for the IRB to complete its review, which can sometimes take a month or two. You should certainly make sure that the IRB process is under way right after your submission, however, so there will be ample time for it to finish before the program officer calls you to congratulate you on the grant you are going to receive.

Do bear in mind that if there are patent risks to human subjects participating in your research, the reviewers and program officers will also be scrutinizing your proposal to determine whether they find the subject protections adequate. If they have concerns about this, they may raise objections that prevent or delay funding, even if the IRB has approved the proposal.

We have dealt here, perhaps excessively, with the procedures for determining that research employing human subjects is designed to protect their interests satisfactorily. Let us conclude this section by returning to a consideration of what is really most important. It is a key professional, ethical, and moral responsibility of any researcher working with human subjects to ensure that no physical, emotional, or social harm come to them as a consequence of the research. This would be true even if there were no Common Rule, no Institutional Review Board, no checkboxes on the proposal cover sheet; these are just mechanisms to help ensure that the subjects will be protected. Protecting your human subjects is by no means the end of your ethical responsibilities as a PI, but it is the most critical one. If you do not sense this viscerally as a compelling, overriding concern, then you don't have the right instincts to do research with human subjects, and should find another line of research to pursue.

Animal Welfare

A considerable amount of biological and biomedical research involves experimentation with living organisms of all sorts. The experimentation is often highly invasive, and frequently results in the death of the organism. A growing societal concern for the well-being of sensate creatures has led to debate about the ethical validity of such research, and to calls for legislation to prohibit or restrict it. Legislators are generally aware, however, of the enormous social benefits that have flowed from biomedical research on animal models – much of modern medicine would not have been possible without it – and feel that it should continue. To address the concerns, and remedy some of the abuses that have been documented, the government has enacted legislation that mandates humane care, handling, and treatment of vertebrate animals used for research and teaching. The Animal Welfare Act, and the regulations that implement it, govern all research on vertebrate animals carried out with the support of research grants awarded by the NIH, the NSF, and other government agencies.

The law requires institutions where research on vertebrate animals occurs to register the relevant research facilities with the U.S. Department of Agriculture, and to establish an Institutional Animal Welfare Assurance with the NIH. The latter Assurance includes the establishment of an Institutional Animal Care and Use Committee (IACUC), which functions similarly to the IRB. The IACUC must review and approve any project involving research on vertebrate animals before a grant can be awarded to support that research.

If an institution applies to NSF for a grant for a project doing research on vertebrate animals, and it has no IACUC (usually because such research is rare at the institution), it can either ask another institution's IACUC to review and approve the project and provide the required oversight during the grant, or else establish an Institutional Animal Welfare Assurance with NSF for that single project, which includes creating its own IACUC for the purpose of the one project. The PI is responsible for checking the box on the cover sheet form to indicate that the research uses vertebrate animals.

The National Academy of Sciences (NAS) has published a *Guide for the Care and Use of Laboratory Animals* that describes in detail the standards and guidelines for treating research animals in a way that complies with the Animal Welfare Act. If your research uses vertebrate animals, you need to study the NAS guide carefully, and abide by it completely.

Conduct and Misconduct in Research

Science is a cumulative enterprise. Every scientist starts from and builds on the results of work that other scientists have done before. This is what gives science the power that it has, and what enables scientific progress. For it to work requires great trust. A researcher has to be able to rely on results that other researchers have reported, or risk at least wasting time and resources on a futile effort, at worst endangering others with false conclusions. The entire scientific community is thus bound together in a network of trust. People who violate that trust betray the community.

As we mentioned at the beginning of this chapter, the standards of scientific conduct that enable the trust that the community requires have long been implicit, unwritten rules. When a series of spectacular violations of the standards came to light a number of years ago, however, the leaders of the scientific community decided that it was essential to spell out the norms of proper scientific conduct explicitly. The major consequence of that decision was a new set of Federal regulations defining misconduct in research, and spelling out procedures for enforcing the regulations and penalties for their violation. A secondary consequence was to raise the awareness of scientists in general of the need to educate their students directly about the ethical standards that all scientists must adhere to, and to include discussion of the standards in books like this one.

The regulations define research misconduct as "fabrication, falsification, or plagiarism in proposing, performing, or reviewing research, or in reporting research results."[5] Let's consider the individual parts of this definition.

You must report the results of your research accurately, completely, and not misleadingly. Violating this principle is *falsification*. Conversely, you must not report results that did not actually emerge from your experimentation or observation, even if you are certain that they must be true. To do so is *fabrication*. As the old formulation has it, you must tell the truth, the whole truth, and nothing but the truth.

You must present, and represent, only your own work as yours. When you rely on or incorporate others' results in your work, as scientists do regularly, you must cite it fully and properly. This is true both for the substantive content of the work itself – the experimental or observational data – and for its written expression in articles and books. Appropriating the work of others without proper attribution is *plagiarism*.

All of these commandments apply to all stages of the research process – writing proposals, conducting research, and reporting the results. Plagiarism in a proposal is as much of a sin as it is in a journal article, and almost as likely to be detected, because the proposal will be read carefully by experts in the field who know the relevant literature.

---

[5] This is the version of the definition published by the Office of Science and Technology Policy in the *Federal Register*. Other documents published by the funding agencies have other versions with slight variations in wording.

Official statements and explanations of these principles all stress that they are not aimed at suppressing honest error, or honest differences in interpretation or judgment of data. Progress in science entails and depends on one scientist detecting an error or a shortcoming in another scientist's results, and formulating a new experiment to resolve it, with ensuing vigorous debate among the parties involved as to the proper interpretation and analysis of the data. Falsification and fabrication are deliberate misrepresentations of the facts. Allegations of misconduct thus require thoroughgoing investigations of intent and state of mind, and careful judgment, before they are confirmed. The responsibility for investigation and judgment rests first with the institutions hosting the research, and secondarily with the funding agencies.

The principles we've discussed were norms of scientific practice long before they were codified into Federal regulations. The penalty for a known violation of them was excommunication – exile from the community of scientists, who could no longer trust the word of the violator and therefore would not read, pay attention to, or rely on his or her reported results. It was only when this sanction proved no longer to be an adequate deterrent that the government issued regulations and instituted enforcement procedures and specified penalties for violations.

Keeping the Funding Agency Informed

From the time you submit your proposal until the agency acts on it, and if the action is a grant, until the grant expires, you are responsible for keeping the agency (meaning the program officer you're dealing with) fully and promptly informed of any significant matters that affect your project, positively or negatively. Some common examples of the kinds of things that may happen are receiving funding from, or being declined by, another source to which you have applied; applying to a funding source that you didn't list in your proposal; an unanticipated need for you or another senior researcher to be absent for an extended period from your institution or from the project site while the project is in progress; the sudden unavailability of an anticipated data source, such as the death of a key research subject or civil strife in the field area you were planning to visit; a natural disaster that hampers your project; or a construction delay that disrupts your schedule. If you're in doubt as to whether you should report a development, do so. Your program officer will always be happy to hear from you (seriously).

Managing Grant Funds Responsibly

If your proposal is successful and the agency awards a grant to fund your research, you will suddenly have authority over and responsibility for the expenditure of a substantial sum of money, probably more than your annual salary. You must be a good and faithful steward of the grant funds, and ensure that they are spent only for purposes that will further the aims of your project. Your SPO, and possibly other people in your department and elsewhere in your institution, will help you manage the grant funds, but as the PI you have the ultimate responsibility. This means you should study carefully any financial reports they send you, and question anything you don't understand.

Obeying the Law

You must obey all of the applicable laws and regulations. It may sound absurdly superfluous to say this, but in fact it requires some conscious awareness on your part. As a PI you become the manager of a workplace, a new and unaccustomed role for many new PIs, and as such you become subject to a whole set of laws that previously may have been outside your concerns. There are laws forbidding discrimination on a number of grounds in hiring people to work on your project; laws prohibiting sexual harassment in the workplace; laws requiring accommodation of handicaps for people working on your project; laws requiring protection from hazardous working conditions; and so on. Your institution has people, in the SPO and elsewhere, who can give you helpful guidance on how to conduct yourself and your project in ways that conform with the law.

The Inspector General

Every Federal agency has an Inspector General. The Office of the Inspector General (OIG) has a mandate to perform audits and investigations of the agency's operations, and to prevent and eliminate waste and fraud. The OIG operates independently of the rest of the agency, reporting directly to the top leadership of the agency and to Congress.

Within NSF, the OIG also has the charge of investigating possible wrongdoing by the people and institutions that receive the funding, and recommending remedies.[6] The wrongdoing may be of a criminal nature, such as embezzlement of grant funds, or it may be misconduct in science of the kind we've been discussing, which legally is an administrative rather than criminal matter, but which the research funding agencies take very seriously.

When someone sees evidence of what they consider to be scientific misconduct, or criminal behavior, on the part of someone working with the support of a research grant from the NSF, the OIG at NSF is the place to report it. NSF employees and people working at the grantee institution *must* report it, and anyone else *may* report it (for example, a reviewer who detects plagiarism in a proposal).

The OIG understands very well the distinction between an allegation and a fact, and has procedures for dealing with allegations and determining their accuracy. If the allegation is of a criminal act, and the OIG sees that there is credible evidence to support it, it will refer the matter to the U.S. Department of Justice for further investigation and action. If it is an allegation of misconduct in science, the OIG will often refer it to the institution, asking them to investigate it and report their findings. Sometimes the OIG will undertake its own investigation if it feels it is called for. If it finds evidence to support the allegation, it will give the subject of the investigation, the person accused of wrongdoing, an opportunity to respond. Finally, if it decides that the evidence supports an allegation of misconduct in science, the OIG will summarize its findings in a report to the deputy director of the NSF. It is up to the deputy director to evaluate the OIG report, make an independent determination of whether scientific misconduct has occurred, and decide the sanctions to be imposed, if any. The subject may appeal the deputy director's decision to the director of the agency, whose decision is final.

---

[6] At NIH, the Office of Research Integrity (ORI) has this responsibility.

Having the OIG around for these purposes is a great boon to the program officer, who is not required nor indeed even allowed to investigate allegations of misconduct. Such allegations frequently come to the program officer's attention first, because he or she is the person the people in the field know and deal with. The program officer's responsibility is simply to immediately refer the matter to the OIG. The ordinary working scientist, on the other hand, may spend an entire career without any contact with the OIG, and be the better for it.

7

The Natural History of a Proposal

I've Written My Proposal – Now What?

After you've invested the large amount of time and effort it took to write a proposal, your work is done for a while, but your worrying is just beginning. That's a natural reaction to the situation, and there's no way to make it go away entirely, but it may help somewhat to understand the process your proposal goes through between the time it leaves your hands and the time, months later, when you learn from the program officer whether you'll receive the grant you've requested or not. In this chapter we'll describe that process as it occurs at one funding agency, the NSF. Other funding agencies will be similar in some respects and different in others; you can learn about their review procedures from their Web sites, and by talking to their program officers.

The Sponsored Projects Office

The first stop on your proposal's journey is the SPO at your institution. Hopefully you've been working with them while developing your proposal, as we have strongly recommended in earlier chapters, so that it doesn't come to them as a complete surprise. It's their job to review the proposal to make sure that it conforms to the requirements of your institution and of the funding agency; that it has received the requisite official approvals; and that the budget is complete and accurate, including fringe benefits and indirect costs at the prescribed levels. They usually need three to five working days (more during holiday seasons) to do all of that, and you have to figure that time into your schedule for getting the proposal to the funding agency by the deadline or target date you're trying to meet.

FastLane makes it easy to transmit your proposal to the SPO, by providing a button labeled "Allow SPO Access." Once you have given the SPO permission to view, edit, and submit the proposal, FastLane automatically generates an e-mail to a designated person there to tell them that your proposal is ready for them to work on. They can then call it up to check it over, make any necessary changes, and submit it to NSF.

Only the SPO has the authority to submit the proposal to NSF. Yes, it's your proposal; you wrote it, and if it results in a grant, the grant will support your work. But from NSF's point of view, the proposal is from your institution, not from you personally, and if NSF awards a grant, it is not to you, but to your institution.[7] NSF expects the SPO to ensure that the institution officially endorses the proposal and will accept a grant and carry out a project under the terms stated in the proposal.

Be sure that the proposal is entirely ready to go before you give the SPO permission to submit it. Do a careful, thorough proofreading, and ask someone else who didn't write the proposal to do the same. When you give the SPO permission, they are going to move as quickly as they can to complete the proposal and submit it. To submit the proposal, they just have to click a button on a screen in FastLane, and they're not likely to check back with you before they do that. Once they have submitted the proposal, it is much more difficult to make any changes in it. If you decide you have to change it after that point, the SPO will have to take special measures to do so, and the delays that will engender may make you miss a deadline.

---

[7] There are provisions for individuals not affiliated with institutions to submit proposals to NSF under certain circumstances. We will not discuss those here. The NSF Web site gives details.

Into the NSF

When the SPO clicks the "Submit" button, the proposal is transmitted electronically to the FastLane server at the NSF. Then several things happen right away. The first is to assign a unique proposal number to your proposal. This is a seven-digit number. The first two digits indicate the fiscal year, and the remaining five digits identify your proposal (if NSF ever gets 100,001 proposals in a single fiscal year, they're going to be in big trouble). FastLane will send an e-mail acknowledging receipt of the proposal and giving the proposal number assigned to it. You should keep a record of the number in some place where you can find it readily; you're likely to need it from time to time in dealing with NSF, although probably not with your program officer, who will associate the proposal with your name rather than its NSF proposal number.

The first real people to see your proposal at NSF are clerical staff in NSF's Proposal Processing Unit (PPU). They check that it complies with NSF's length limits, and that it has no appendices (unless it is in response to a program announcement that requires an appendix of some sort). They report violations to the program officer to whom the proposal is directed. The program officer may or may not get in touch with you to explain the problem if this happens. If the program officer does nothing, the proposal will be automatically logged out of the system unreviewed, and you will receive a notification of this by e-mail. If the program officer contacts you, you may be able to replace the proposal with one that conforms to the rules in time for a prompt review – or you may not. So don't take a chance of wasting your work; *obey the length limits.*

After your proposal passes the input check, the PPU prints out a couple of paper copies of it and delivers them to the primary program to which the proposal is assigned, according to the selection you made in completing the cover sheet form that we discussed in Chapter 5. A program officer looks it over to be sure it's correctly assigned. If the program officer feels that another program should have primary responsibility for the proposal, he or she will take it to a program officer in that other program for discussion and a joint decision about assignment, and will transfer the proposal to the other program and notify you that this has happened. Also, if you have requested a secondary assignment of the proposal to another program, or if the program officer decides independently that another program should participate in the review, he or she will take the proposal to the other program and invite them to join in.

When the assignment of the proposal is definite, the program staff log it in to the program, which means entering a certain amount of data and generating a "jacket," a cardboard folder holding a physical copy of the proposal and associated documents, and files it along with the other active current proposals. The proposal is then ready to enter the review process.

The Review Process

As we said in Chapter 5, NSF programs vary in the proposal review procedures they use. Some use only ad hoc reviewers, some use advisory panels, and some use both. For the sake of this discussion, we will describe a program that uses both ad hoc reviewers and a panel to review proposals.

Ad Hoc Review. The program officer selects about six ad hoc reviewers for the proposal, perhaps more if the topic is unusually wide-ranging or multidisciplinary. This is a big job, by the time one does it for the eighty or so proposals that make up a round of review, and a big responsibility, one that NSF program officers take very seriously. They want to elicit a fair, balanced, and thorough review of every proposal, finding reviewers who are recognized experts in the field of the proposed research, who have no conflicts of interest in evaluating the PI's work, and who fairly represent the spectrum of opinions on controversial topics (which most good research topics are). And they must do this across the full range of specialties and subdisciplines that their program supports, which often represent completely disjoint research communities.

Program officers make use of several sources of information in identifying a good set of ad hoc reviewers for a proposal. Many maintain a database of reviewers on the NSF computer system, with associated descriptors indicating their research specialties. Professional societies sometimes make available lists of their members, with some coding of specialization. Commercial abstracting services available over the Internet allow someone to search on a research topic and find authors who have written on that topic. Program officers try to keep up with the major journals and professional meetings in their field, and note who is writing and talking about what. The list of References Cited included with the proposal is an important source, as we mentioned in Chapter 5. Anyone asked to review a proposal is given the opportunity to name other qualified reviewers, and that provides lots of helpful suggestions. And, as we said, the PI may send a list of suggested reviewers along with the proposal, and the program officer will gladly select some names from that list.

It can be a helpful introduction to the world of proposals and grants to review a proposal or two yourself before you write one. Program officers are always on the lookout for new reviewers, so if you would like to review a proposal, you can contact a program officer in your field and volunteer to do so. The best way to do this, probably, is to send an e-mail message. Give enough information about yourself to enable the program officer to determine your qualifications and enter your name in the reviewer database – mailing address, e-mail address, institutional affiliation, highest degree and where you got it, and a fairly specific description of the research areas you specialize in, listing a few of your recent publications. If you just say "anthropology" or "computer science," the program officer won't know which of the multitude of varied proposals in those broad areas you're competent to review. Of course, if you publish a journal article or give a talk at a major professional meeting, you may be asked to review a proposal whether you volunteer or not.

Having identified a set of appropriate reviewers, the program officer sends them invitations to review the proposal. Reviewers are able to receive the proposal electronically or to request NSF to send them a paper copy of it. In either case, the program officer asks them to return a review of the proposal on FastLane within about four weeks.

For programs that don't have panels, the ad hoc reviews are the entire external input to the program officer's funding decisions. If a program uses both ad hoc reviews and an advisory panel, the panel will have an opportunity to see and comment on the ad hoc reviews during its discussion of a proposal.

The Panel. The meeting of the advisory panel (for programs that use them) is the anchor point of the review cycle. The program and the panelists all start preparing for the meeting some weeks in advance. When all of the proposals to be reviewed are in hand, the program officer goes through them and assigns them to the panelists who will have primary responsibility for reviewing them. The assignments are mainly based on expertise, with panelists reviewing proposals in areas they have worked in or close to, but the program officer also has to balance out the load, to try to ensure that each panelist has roughly an equivalent amount of work. Depending on how the program organizes its panel review, each proposal may be assigned to two or three panelists to prepare written reviews, and perhaps one or two others as discussants.

After the assignments are complete, at least a month ahead of the panel meeting, the program officer sends them out to the panelists. The panelists have access to a special module of FastLane that allows them to view, and review, all of the proposals on the panel's agenda for the current cycle. The panelists commit a significant amount of time and effort to preparing for the panel meeting, often writing careful reviews of a dozen or more proposals in the weeks before the meeting.

A week or two before the meeting, the panelists see the ad hoc reviews that the program has received for the proposals on the agenda. The program usually asks the panelists to complete their own reviews of a proposal before looking at what the ad hoc reviewers have said about it, to ensure that they give their independent opinion, but the panel will discuss the ad hoc reviews as part of the discussion of each proposal, so the panelists need to read them in advance.

The panel meeting usually takes place at NSF, although it can be elsewhere. Sometimes a program will schedule a panel meeting just before or just after a major professional meeting, in the same locale, so that the panelists can attend both on the same trip, or the panel may meet at a panelist's home institution. Most regular NSF programs have one or two panel meetings a year, anchoring their one or two annual review cycles. A panel meeting normally runs for two or three days, depending on the number of proposals on the agenda.

The panel has to evaluate the full set of proposals under review. The evaluation procedure may vary among the proposals, however. Some proposals by this stage in the cycle may have received very negative reviews from ad hoc reviewers and from the assigned panelists. If the program officer is satisfied that the written reviews already in hand provide ample justification to decline a proposal, and adequate feedback to the PI who submitted it, he or she may suggest that the panel dispense with discussing it, and if no panelist objects, that ends the matter.

Most of the proposals will survive this triage, and will come up for active discussion by the panel. A typical panel discussion of a proposal will begin with the panelists who were assigned to the proposal presenting their take on it. Then a panelist will read or summarize the ad hoc reviews of the proposal, and comment on them. A general discussion follows, in which all the panelists may participate. The aim of the discussion is for the panel to converge on a consensus evaluation of the proposal. That doesn't always happen, but for a surprisingly large percentage of the proposals it does.

When the discussion reaches a consensus, or it becomes clear that it won't, the program officer calls an end to it and asks the panel for an overall rating of the proposal on a standardized scale, to help in ranking it relative to other proposals later when it comes time to make funding decisions. Then someone who has been designated for the task prepares a written summary of the panel discussion, which becomes part of the review documentation for the proposal, and part of the feedback to the PI. The panel summary addresses the two major review criteria, the scientific merit of the proposal and its broader impacts, highlighting the proposal's major strengths and weaknesses. It includes commentary on the written reviews, mentioning points in them that the panel agreed or disagreed with, and concludes with a recommendation as to the action the program should take on the proposal.

Depending on the program officer's preferences, the panel may also engage in explicitly ranking all of the proposals discussed, usually after completing the discussions of all of the individual proposals. At NSF, however, the panel's role is officially advisory; the program officer is responsible for the final funding recommendations.

The panel's primary job is to evaluate proposals, and that's how it spends most of its time. An NSF advisory panel, however, also fills a broader role, advising the program and the Foundation on the present and coming needs in the fields of science that the program serves, and on the impacts, good and bad, of the policies and practices that the program and the NSF employ. Sometimes the program officer will contact panelists informally to sound them out on some matter, and sometimes the panel will devote part of a meeting to discussing these broader issues. That part of the meeting is called the "open meeting," because unlike the panel sessions devoted to proposal review, which are confidential and closed to everyone except panelists and NSF personnel, the open panel session can in principle be attended by anyone. The program officer can often make good use of the comments made in the open meeting when preparing internal reports on the program's strategic planning.

The Program Officer. The period right after the panel meeting is an intense one for the program officer, who has to act as promptly as possible on all of the proposals under review. Program officers differ in how they manage their work at this time; the scenario we describe here is one possible model, but don't be surprised if your program officer does it differently.

For something like half of the proposals reviewed, it will be clear from the ad hoc reviews and the panel discussion that there is no likelihood that they will lead to a grant. The program officer's first step is to decline the proposals in this group. Declining a proposal requires writing up a document that summarizes the reasons for the declination; making sure that the written reviews, from ad hoc reviewers and from panelists, and the panel summary are ready to transmit to the PI; and notifying the PI, usually by e-mail. As soon as the PI receives the notification, he or she may log onto FastLane and read the reviews and the panel summary. NSF keeps the reviewers anonymous, and the program officer has to check each review carefully before making it available to the PI, to be sure that it does not contain information that would identify the reviewer. Otherwise the PI sees all of the review material that the program officer considered in deciding to decline the proposal.

Next the program officer turns to the proposals emerging from the review with the very highest rankings, the few proposals (maybe 10 percent of the full set) that are the strongest candidates for funding on the basis of the review. He or she rereads the proposal enough to get a firm concept of the project, studies the reviews and the panel

summary carefully, notes any special factors relating to the funding
decision (e.g., that the proposal is a renewal request, or from a new
PI), and analyzes the budget in detail, deciding whether the needs of
the project justify the amounts requested in each line item, possibly
arriving at a reduced overall budget figure for the project.

Based on this study and analysis, the program officer selects an initial set of proposals to fund, deciding for each an appropriate budget
amount, project duration, and start date. The program officer may at
this point discuss the initial funding plans with his or her division
director. Then it is time to contact the PIs to discuss these matters, by
telephone if at all possible (a phone call is the best medium for such
discussions). If the budget, start date, or project duration the program officer is considering differs from what the proposal requested,
the program officer and PI have to come to terms about the changes.
This interaction is sometimes called "negotiating a revised budget,"
but it's not really a negotiation as the term is normally understood,
at least not usually. It's too one-sided. The program officer tells the
PI what the program is prepared to offer, and the PI has to decide
whether to accept a grant and undertake the project under the revised terms. There is, however, an opportunity for the PI to make a
case for restoring part or all of the original budget request, if there are
strong and persuasive reasons for doing so that the program officer
has not already taken into account. It won't usually happen, but it
doesn't hurt to try. The PI can also try to make a case for changes in
the start date or project duration the program is offering, if there are
reasons to do so.

If the PI had the same or other proposals pending at other funding
agencies while NSF was reviewing the current proposal, the program
officer will want to know the status of those applications. If any of
them are being funded, or are likely to be, that may have a direct
impact on NSF's action. The program officer may check this with
the PI, or with program officers at the other agencies reviewing the
project.

When the PI and the program officer have agreed on a budget,
if it is changed from the budget request submitted with the original
proposal, the PI needs to submit a revised budget. This has to come
through the PI's institution, which needs to know that an award is
likely, and in what amount, and when, and needs to approve the

changes in the proposal that it had endorsed. If the requested budget is reduced by more than 10 percent, the PI also has to provide NSF a revised statement of the project work plan. This is a brief document, usually less than a page, which states what elements of the originally proposed project may not be accomplished as a consequence of the budget reductions. The PI and the program officer should confer closely on this statement and agree on its content before the PI submits it formally. The program officer may have definite ideas, based on the review, as to which components of the project are of lower priority, and the PI should conform to these or else convince the program officer that another kind of reduction in the project is better.

At this point, the program officer has not yet contacted the PIs of proposals on which no funding decision has been made. The program is working within a budget, and the program officer has to keep careful track of the program's financial commitments. This means determining the final budget amounts for the projects that have already been selected for funding; finding out what is happening at other agencies that are reviewing counterpart proposals to the ones the program is considering; conferring with other NSF programs who are co-reviewing and may co-fund certain proposals, or may be sources of additional funding for some projects; exploring possibilities for expanding the program's budget by tapping into reserve funds; and so on. Because it would be grossly irresponsible for a program officer to lead a PI to believe that funding might be forthcoming and then have to decline the proposal after all, the program officer is careful not to contact PIs about possible grants until he or she knows the resources are available to fund their proposals. PIs whose proposals are "in the middle," neither clear declines nor clear awards, thus have to wait longer to learn NSF's response than other PIs. As the program's financial picture becomes clearer, the program officer will continue to select additional projects for funding as long as the money holds out. We discussed in Chapter 5 the variety of considerations that the program officer may employ in making funding decisions among this group of proposals that all warrant support but cannot all receive it because of the limits of the program's budget.

So when exactly will you learn the fate of your NSF proposal? If a panel participates in reviewing the proposal, the key to the answer is the date the panel meets, which you can find out from the NSF

Web site or from the program officer. The earliest that you can expect to hear anything is two to three weeks after the panel meeting, and that soon, the news is likely to be bad, because as we said the clear declinations usually go out first. Within a month or less after the panel meeting, the program officer is ordinarily in a position to begin talking to PIs about possible grants, and those conversations are likely to continue for another month or more. If you haven't heard anything for about six weeks after the panel meeting, it's reasonable to send your program officer an e-mail to check on the status of your proposal, but don't be surprised to get a brief reply that it's still under consideration but no decision has been made yet. You can consider this moderately good news; it probably means your proposal is in the top half of those reviewed in the current round, and still has a chance for funding. In any case, the NSF standard is to notify every PI of the outcome of the review within six months after the deadline or target date for proposal submission. If the six months passes with no word from NSF, you're entitled to complain, first to your program officer, and if you don't get a satisfactory response from that, to the program officer's division director.

Under some circumstances the program officer may have to, or may choose to, defer a funding decision on a proposal for a more extended period. NSF requires that there be at least three written reviews of a proposal before a program acts on it, and occasionally a proposal will reach the decision time in the review cycle without having received the requisite number of reviews. If this happens, the program officer has to send reminder requests to the original reviewers or solicit new reviews, and either solution takes additional time. It can also happen that a program officer would like to fund a particular proposal, and cannot within the currently available program budget, but feels there may be some opportunity to do so later, perhaps because some other proposal selected for funding gets support from another agency, or perhaps in the subsequent round of review the proposal may end up just above the funding threshold rather than just below it. When one of these situations arises, the program officer should let the PI know that there will be a delay, and what the reasons for it are.

When the program officer decides to put a proposal forward for a grant, and has reached agreement with the PI on the terms of the grant (budget, duration, start date, any revisions in the plan of work), there's some paperwork to do. The program officer has to check the Project Summary in the proposal for accuracy, completeness, and clarity, and to edit it if necessary to make it suitable for public display on the NSF Web site. He or she has to check all the reviews to ensure that they don't reveal the identities of the reviewers, and to highlight salient points for entry into the NSF database, such as any involvement of foreign countries in the project. Most importantly, the program officer has to write a document called a "Form 7," an internal NSF document that analyzes the reviews of the proposal and sets out the basis for the decision to fund the project, with responses to any significant criticisms of the proposal that appear in the reviews.

Although the program officer makes the critical decision as to whether a proposal will be funded or not, the program officer does not and cannot award grants. The program officer's funding decisions go forward in the form of recommendations to be reviewed, endorsed, and acted on by other NSF offices, two in particular: the program officer's division director, and the NSF Division of Grants and Agreements (DGA). The division director must concur with the award recommendation, which usually happens within a week or so if the program officer has provided adequate documentation for the recommendation. Then the recommendation goes forward to the DGA, which checks it thoroughly for conformity to NSF policies and requirements, and issues the actual grant. The whole process normally takes at least six weeks, from the time the program officer puts forward the award recommendation until DGA notifies the institution that the grant is official.

During the interval between the program officer's recommendation and the actual grant award – while NSF is doing the work necessary to make the grant – the institution can provide the PI with advance funds to get the project started – for example, to purchase equipment and supplies that will be needed from the beginning of the research – and can recover those funds from the grant when it arrives. The only limitation is that the fund advances must be made no more than ninety days before the starting date of the grant. The institution is prudent to check with the program officer that the award is in process, and expected in less than ninety days, before advancing funds.

Whenever NSF completes its action on a proposal, whether it is to award a grant or to decline the proposal, it makes the full text of all of the reviews of the proposal, and the summary of the panel's discussion if there was one, available to the PI right away. The PI receives special access to FastLane to read them. NSF grants this access to no one other than the PI – not to the institution, not to Co-PIs, not to anyone. The PI can choose who to share the reviews with. PIs who receive grants are well advised to study their reviews as carefully as those whose proposals are declined; reviewers often have valuable suggestions to offer that can improve the project markedly.

Working with Your Program Officer

Applicants sometimes find it hard to know how to relate to a program officer at a funding agency, what is the proper etiquette in dealing with him or her. An entire book[8] has been written on the premise that the secret to successful grant-getting is to establish the right relationship with a program officer (in fairness, that book addresses an audience of fundraisers for nonprofit cultural, charitable, and social action organizations, rather than scientists). Program officers at the NSF and other government agencies that fund research reject this notion. Like any humans, they like some people better than others, but they base their funding decisions on factors we've already discussed in great detail, not on their personal likes and dislikes.

Program officers simply hope that the people they deal with in the research community will treat them as respected colleagues. They do not respond well to obsequious deference or to flattery, nor do they appreciate being badgered and berated. If you are a member of a college or university faculty, the etiquette that guides you in dealing with your colleagues on a daily basis will work fine with program officers. They do hope you understand how busy they are, and appreciate your contacting them in a way that allows for an efficient reply – e-mail for questions with short definite answers, phone calls for matters that call for a more extended, discursive response. And you can often save yourself and your program officer some time by

[8] *Successful Grantsmanship: A Guerilla Guide to Raising Money*, by Susan L. Golden, San Francisco: Jossey-Bass, 1997.

checking the agency Web site first, to see if it has an answer to your question.

You may have a personal or collegial relationship with a program officer from an earlier time, before that person became a program officer. It's fine to maintain a friendly relationship, but you need to recognize that as a program officer your friend is working under a new set of constraints, and you should not expect special treatment or extra attention compared to others who did not have a prior connection with the program officer. If your relationship with the program officer is close enough to create a conflict of interest for him or her, according to the agency's rules, then he or she will have to refrain altogether from dealing with your proposal, and will have to have a substitute handle it.

8

"We Are Happy/Sorry to Inform You..."

Your wait is over. The funding agency has given you the news, good or bad, about what is going to happen with your proposal. What do you do next? Well, of course, that depends on what the news was. In this chapter, we'll look at each of the three possible outcomes – an award, a declination, or a deferred decision.

"... You're Going to Get a Grant!"

Congratulations. This is a very significant accomplishment. The competition for research grants is very stiff, and your proposal has been selected for funding among those submitted by some of the best scientists in your field. The good news is an immediate boost to your spirits and a long-term boost to your chances to do some outstanding research with the resources you need. There are several things you should do right away.

1. *Celebrate!* What better occasion for a party? You may as well do this first thing, because chances are you won't have time for it later, once you get heavily into your research. Just remember to share the good news, and the celebration, with all of the people who helped you to prepare and submit your proposal, and to endure the anxious wait for the results. There are probably more of them than occur to you immediately, so give it some careful thought to be sure that you include everyone – colleagues, students, support staff in your

department and others, your Sponsored Projects Office, your administration, family, and friends. Not only is it the polite and decent thing to do, but it also makes it easier the next time you have to ask for their help, which you will.

2. *Visit your sponsored projects office.* There is some business that you need to take care of right away, such as setting up the necessary funding accounts. You also need to get a clear understanding of what the people in the SPO expect from you, immediately and on a continuing basis; they may ask you for periodic financial reports, or receipts for expenditures, or for data about the personnel working on your project, or whatever. Your life will be a lot easier for the duration of your project, and beyond, if you are able to set up a good working relationship with your SPO at the outset.

If you need or want advance funding to help get your project started during the six to eight weeks or more before the actual grant arrives, this is the time to request it. The SPO may need to seek confirmation of your proposal's status from the funding agency first, but they can usually act very quickly to set up an account with funds you can access to purchase equipment and so forth.

Larger research institutions often have staff people at the department level who work on proposals and grants. If you are fortunate enough to have access to such a person, you will also want to sit down with her or him to work out the administrative procedures you will be following.

3. *Study the material the funding agency provides.* The agency that is making the grant to support your research has a set of procedures and regulations that affect PIs. You probably haven't had the motivation to study these earlier, but now you need to. The NSF, for example, summarizes key sections of its voluminous *Grants Policy Manual* into a booklet called "Grant General Conditions," which you can read on the NSF Web site. Reading it is a little like reading a digest of the traffic code, or instructions from the IRS, but you should still make the effort to read and understand it, because it spells out your institution's principal responsibilities as a recipient of NSF funds (what the document calls an "awardee"), and many of those affect your responsibilities as a PI. Knowing what it says can help avoid surprises, possibly unpleasant ones, later.

4. *Start making preliminary arrangements.* If this is a new project, there are probably going to be a number of things you need to do to get things started, and this is the time to start doing them. If you will be acquiring new equipment with the grant funds, this usually takes a certain amount of lead time, and you should begin the process. The advance funding that you can get through your SPO, as we mentioned earlier, may be essential for the purpose. You will probably be hiring a graduate student as a research assistant, and unless you already have someone firmly in mind and committed to accepting the job, you have some recruiting to do. If your project involves any travel during the first few months, making the arrangements well in advance will often get you substantial savings on the fares. Getting stocked up with necessary materials and supplies and arranging services such as a telephone connection before the official start date of the grant will give your project a good head start.

5. *Respond promptly to requests from the funding agency.* The program officer and the office responsible for actually awarding the grant (at NSF, the Division of Grants and Agreements) are working on your proposal during the period between the time you've learned that a grant is forthcoming and the official start date of the grant. They often discover a need for additional information, or to resolve some apparent discrepancy in the proposal, and will contact you or your SPO to find out what they need to in order to proceed toward making the grant. If you get such a request, it is very much in your interest to respond to it right away. The agency has probably suspended work on your proposal until they hear back from you, and if they have to suspend work for too long, it may lead to delaying the start date of your grant. If you're away from your office, be sure to check your messages regularly, in case the agency is trying to reach you.

6. *Know and meet your ethical responsibilities.* We devoted a full chapter to this topic, and won't reiterate it here. We mention it in this context because the principles that guide ethical research may seem rather abstract when you are simply reading about them or discussing them with others, but when you embark on your project they are very real and seriously important rules to follow. If your research involves human subjects or vertebrate animals, now is the time to make the concrete provisions for their welfare.

7. *Do your research!* Finally you've reached the point you've been working toward so hard for so long – a chance to do some interesting science. Relax and enjoy it; you've earned it.

"... Your Proposal Has Been Declined"

No matter how much you have tried to prepare yourself for the possibility, learning that your proposal has been declined is a sharp disappointment. The work and the hope that you invested in preparing and submitting your proposal are not going to enjoy the reward of a grant, at least not this time around. Disappointment is inevitable, but there are a number of constructive things you can do to react to it.

1. *Keep your perspective.* Some 80 percent of all proposals are declined, including proposals from some of the best-known names in your field. Just about every active researcher who seeks external grants has had proposals declined at one time or another, often multiple times. Given the number of good scientists working, and the limits on the grant funds available, it's inevitable. You're in good company.

2. *Glance at the reviews.* When you first get access to the reviews and the panel summary, you should look through them quickly to get the gist of the commentary. Don't sit down to study them carefully yet, because you're not in the right frame of mind when you've first learned that your proposal has been declined. You're likely to get hung up on a particular criticism that you find unfair or ill-informed, and waste time and emotional energy fretting about it.

3. *Later, study the reviews.* After a day or two, when the initial emotional reaction to the declination has subsided and you can do so more dispassionately, go back and read the reviews and the panel summary carefully. Try to discern critical themes that appear in more than one review, as these are likely to have been especially influential in the decision to decline your proposal. Begin thinking systematically about your intellectual reactions to the reviewers' criticisms: which ones do you find persuasive, which ones misguided, which ones result from a misunderstanding of the proposal? Look through the panel summary for the panel's comments about the written reviews; sometimes the panel will reject a criticism that it finds misguided or unfair. If you

see a comment like that, the chances are very high that the program officer also dismissed the criticism in making the decision to decline the proposal.

As you analyze the reviews, consider how you should respond to each criticism and suggestion. Those you find persuasive may lead you to make changes in the design of your project. Comments that reflect reviewers' misunderstanding of your proposal indicate that you need to revise the proposal in ways that should prevent similar misunderstandings the next time around. And some comments, after careful consideration, you should simply ignore. Reviewers are not omniscient, and they do make wrong and even boneheaded comments sometimes. You need to retain the self-confidence to decide that in a particular instance, you are right and the reviewer isn't. It may well be that the program officer had the same opinion; this is something you will want to check on a little later, when you talk to the program officer.

4. *Discuss the reviews with someone.* Share your reviews, and your reactions to them, with a colleague who is knowledgeable in your area of science and whose opinions you respect. This may be someone at your institution, or someone located elsewhere; what's important is that it be someone who knows enough about what you're doing that he or she could have served as a reviewer of your proposal, and who will give you the time and attention for an in-depth discussion of the reviews. You need to bounce your ideas, and your reactions to the reviewers' comments, off of someone with a different perspective, and without the ego involvement in your project that you have developed. It will be natural for your colleague to want to be sympathetic and supportive, and to side with you against your critics, but the consultation will be more useful if you can both surmount this tendency, and have a really frank discussion.

5. *Talk to the program officer.* When you have a clear understanding of the reviews, have formulated your own considered responses to them, and discussed same with a knowledgeable colleague, call or e-mail the program officer. Program officers don't give all reviewers' comments and criticisms equal weight in making funding decisions, and it will help you to learn which criticisms were the most salient in the decision to decline the proposal. If you found some of the criticisms foolish or misguided or unfair, ask whether they were taken

seriously in the final evaluation of the proposal. Don't try to argue with the program officer or rebut the criticisms in this conversation; you're simply trying to gather information about the review of your proposal, and the decision to decline it, that has not already been made available to you.

Sometimes there are no significant criticisms, the reviewers really liked your proposal, and it was still declined. This unfortunately happens more often than it should, and it is painful for program officers when it does. The reason is almost always that the program simply doesn't have enough money in its budget to fund all of the well-reviewed proposals, so the program officer has to make some hard choices and decline some of them that he or she would be happy to support if the funds were available. Those hard choices entail making some priority judgments about what the program should support, judgments that the program officer may make on a variety of grounds, as we have seen in earlier chapters.

If this seems to be your situation – your proposal has strongly positive reviews and no significant criticisms – you need to get some sense from the program officer as to why you didn't reach the funding threshold, and more importantly, whether you can expect to have a better chance the next time around. A good program officer should give you a candid and rather specific answer to this question, rather than just offering you generic encouragement to try again. Perhaps, for example, you are working in an area that the program is already supporting heavily, and the program officer feels that other areas of the program's responsibility require higher-priority attention for a while. Of course, if you argue with what the program officer tells you, you will immediately elicit the response that it's fine for you to go ahead and revise and resubmit your proposal if you want to, which is true. But since your time and energy are in finite supply, it may be more useful to you to know a realistic estimate of your prospects before you undertake the effort of revising the proposal. And you must revise it before you can resubmit it; NSF does not allow the resubmission of a proposal that has already been reviewed.

6. *Revise and resubmit.* By the time you've studied the reviews, determined your reactions to them, and discussed same with a colleague and with the program officer, you have a pretty clear idea as

to whether you can modify your proposal, and perhaps your project, in ways that respond effectively to the well-founded criticisms from the reviewers. Once in a while people find a criticism so serious, and so insurmountable, that they decide to abandon the project, but usually after a period of thought and analysis they see ways to meet the criticisms and improve the proposal. You've now reached the point of deciding what you want to do. You may find advice in the reviews; if reviewers find your basic idea exciting, but spot flaws in the project design or in the proposal that need to be fixed before the project can succeed, they may advise you to revise and resubmit the proposal. This encouragement is worth taking seriously, but the decision is yours. If you have satisfied yourself that it makes sense to do so, you're ready to go ahead and revise the proposal, and resubmit it for another round of review.[9]

You need to consider the timing. Sometimes there isn't a lot of time between the day you learn that your proposal is being declined and the deadline or target date for the next round of review. You really need to go through the process of thinking and discussing we've just outlined before you revise your proposal, and you need to allow yourself enough time to do the revisions carefully and well. It won't take as long to revise the proposal as it did to write it in the first place, but if you do it in a rush and end up with a half-baked job, you're setting yourself up for another disappointing review. It might be better to let one deadline or target date pass, and aim for the following one, to allow time to produce a really strong revised proposal. However, life isn't always that generous with time; you may have good reasons why it's urgent to get your proposal back on track for review as quickly as possible. Check with the program officer about how much time you have to get the proposal in for the next round of review. Sometimes program officers can allow you a little leeway on a target date, if there was some delay on the agency's end in notifying you of the declination and giving you access to the reviews.

[9] The procedures we discuss in this section are specific to the NSF. Other agencies handle revised and resubmitted proposals in different ways. Check with a program officer about the appropriate procedures before you begin to revise and resubmit your proposal.

In writing your revised proposal, think of it as a new, self-contained document. That is, don't just insert your replies to the reviewers' comments into the appropriate sections of your previous proposal and send it in again. Some of the reviewers of the revised proposal will be new ones, who didn't see your previous proposal, and you don't want to make them feel like they've come in on the middle of someone else's conversation. And the reviewers who did see the previous proposal want to see evidence that you've actually given serious thought to the criticisms and questions they raised, and incorporated your considered responses to them into the design of your project. What you need to do is to rewrite the proposal, or the relevant portions of it, in such a way that the valid criticisms and questions about the previous proposal simply no longer apply.

Also be sure to take note of things the reviewers praised about your previous proposal. These are strengths you can build on. Perhaps you can expand the scope of activities in your project that reviewers particularly liked, at the expense of those that did not excite their enthusiasm. At least make sure that those elements retain a conspicuous place in the revised proposal.

The revisions don't have to be limited to what reviewers said. You have probably had your own second and third thoughts about what you wrote in your previous proposal during the months since you sent it in. You may have been pursuing the research to the extent you could without a grant, and have come up with new results that bear on your project in important ways. Let the revised proposal reflect the development of your own thinking about the project, as well as your responses to the reviews.

Your revised proposal will be reviewed just like a new proposal. The program officer, and the reviewers who saw the previous proposal, will know that it is a resubmission, of course, but it will compete on equal terms with all of the other proposals in the next round of review – the fact that your previous proposal was declined is neither a black mark nor a extra boost in the review of the revised version.

The program officer is likely to select a mixed set of reviewers for the revised proposal, including some who saw the previous version and some who did not. The latter group will not know that the proposal is a resubmission unless the proposal itself says so. There is a frustrating but real possibility that some reviewers who are new to your proposal will raise new criticisms that didn't arise in the previous review, possibly even urging changes that would restore something you removed or amended from the earlier proposal in response to the first set of reviews. This can be highly annoying, but you should just recognize it as part of an admittedly imperfect process. Chances are, the program officer has noticed it, too, and will think that the discrepancy in the reviews lessens the force of the criticism involved.

The revised proposal can include a list of suggested reviewers, like any proposal, and you can use that list to request that the author of some specific review of the previous proposal not be asked to review the revised one. You won't know the reviewer's identity, but you can identify the one you mean by quoting the first line or so of the review. Use the opportunity judiciously, to exclude a reviewer or two who appear to oppose the fundamental premise of your project, who wouldn't like it no matter how it was revised or presented; or a reviewer whose comments reflect a basic lack of understanding of your science or of your proposal. Don't ask to exclude every reviewer who made any criticisms, or the program officer won't take you seriously.

Is it worth it? Can revised proposals succeed? In a word, yes. There is of course no guarantee that the revised proposal will be funded, even if you successfully respond to all of the criticisms, but they succeed often enough to make it worth your time and effort to revise the proposal and resubmit it. If you talk to colleagues who have experience in submitting proposals and getting grants, it's likely that many of them have had to revise a proposal, perhaps more than once, before finally receiving funding for it.

For more extensive advice on dealing with declination, I recommend the book *The Research Funding Guidebook: Getting It, Managing It, and Renewing It,* by Joanne B. Ries and Carl G. Leukefeld, published in 1998 by Sage Publications. It has a long, excellent chapter on the topic. The book is based in the context of NIH proposals and grants (in the same sense that this book is based in an NSF context), but applicants to other agencies will also find its advice relevant and helpful.

7. *Reconsideration.* It may happen that a PI whose proposal has been declined studies the reviews, talks them over with the program

officer, and concludes that in this instance the review process failed – the reviewers, or some of them, had an *a priori* bias against the PI or the project, or revealed by their comments that they lacked an adequate understanding of the science in the proposal to pass judgment on it, or in some other way the reviews did not constitute the full and fair evaluation of the proposal that NSF promises to every PI.

To deal with circumstances like this, NSF offers PIs a type of appeal process called "reconsideration." The reconsideration process brings the Assistant Director or Office Head – the program officer's boss's boss – into the act, to examine the record of the proposal's review and the decision to decline it and to determine whether the review fell short of NSF standards. The NSF *Grant Proposal Guide* spells out the procedures and timetables for reconsideration.

The reconsideration mechanism is a valuable safeguard for PIs, to deal with the (thankfully rare) situation when the program officer has made a significant error in dealing with a proposal and will neither admit it nor do anything about it. However, you should invoke it only as a last resort, when the situation is so egregious that you have no other alternative. In most cases, you are better off to revise and resubmit the proposal. The reconsideration process takes enough time that it will cause you to miss a round of review that you might otherwise have participated in, and even if it does reveal an error in the review, it may not result in your project being funded, because there may not be any funds remaining in the budget for it (the *Grant Proposal Guide* makes this point explicitly). A reconsideration request reflects a breakdown in trust, communication, and collegiality between the PI and the program officer, and so is in a sense the "nuclear option." Use it if you feel you must, but be aware of the gravity of doing so.

"... We have to Hold on to Your Proposal for a While"

The third logically possible outcome of the review of your proposal is that nothing happens, at least not right away. This is in some ways more frustrating than a declination, which is at least a definite event, but there are reasons for it that the program officer will explain to you.

The program officer may defer a decision on your proposal either by necessity or by choice. "Necessity" covers cases where it is not possible for the program officer to act on your proposal for some reason related to NSF policy, most usually an insufficient number of reviews. NSF requires at least three written reviews for any action on a proposal. Program officers make valiant efforts to assure that every proposal will have at least three reviews by the time in the review cycle when it is time to act on the proposals, and most of them do. Sometimes, however, enough reviewers fail to respond to a particular proposal that by decision time there are just two, or one, or no reviews in hand. Program officers make no inferences about the quality of a proposal from the absence of reviews, but they can't act on it until they have three or more, and getting the requisite number is going to take some extra time. If this happens to your proposal, the program officer should tell you about it, and should give you an idea of how long it will be before you can expect a decision.

The more interesting circumstance is when the program officer chooses to defer decision on your proposal. This is a mechanism the program officer may use when your proposal is right at the funding "margin" – well enough reviewed to warrant funding, but with a lower priority than some of the other proposals it is in competition with, which are going to use up the available budget for the current round of review. The program officer wants to ensure a consistent level of quality in funded proposals from one round of review to the next, a level that doesn't vary with the number of proposals that happen to come in for a particular review cycle, which can vary considerably. If there were a larger than usual number of proposals in the round of review in which your proposal was considered, the program officer may feel that your proposal may fare better competitively in the next round, if the number of proposals drops back down to a more normal level.

If the program officer suggests this to you, it's usually a good idea to agree, although you should understand clearly that there is no guarantee that you will get funded in the next round. Your alternative is to have the proposal declined, and revise and resubmit it. That's more work, but might have the possible advantage that you could improve the review of the proposal in the next round, and thus its funding priority. You should discuss with the program officer whether the reviews offer some clear indications of improvements that should be made in the proposal. Chances are, the program officer has already considered this, and has decided that you are just as well off to wait as to revise and resubmit, but you want to be clear on the point. The program officer may offer to let you see the reviews and panel summary, so that you can make your own judgment about how likely it is that you can revise the proposal as needed in the time available.

NSF has a standard of six months for action on all proposals. If the decision on your proposal is deferred, it will almost certainly be longer than six months before it occurs, so the program officer has the responsibility to explain the situation to you clearly and get your agreement to the delay. You don't have to agree, but if you don't, the action will be either a declination or a withdrawal of the proposal, so you have to decide whether you are willing to wait extra time for the possibility, perhaps not a large one, of favorable action.

9

Managing Your Grant

When your proposal turns into a grant, you turn into an administrator as well as a scientist. Along with conducting your research, you also have to manage the grant. This isn't too onerous a job, but it does require you to pay attention to some matters that you may not have had to worry about before, and to do some things that may be new to your roster of duties. In this chapter, we'll discuss some of the managerial responsibilities that come along with a research grant.

Managing a Research Project

As the PI of a research project funded by a government agency, you are in effect the head of a small business. It's up to you to make sure that you and your staff are working productively, that you have on hand the materials and supplies you need to do the work, that you are using resources wisely and efficiently, that you are staying on schedule and within budget, and that you are reporting as necessary to others who have a stake in your research, including your institution and the funding agency. Fortunately, your institution will take care of some aspects of the management for you, such as meeting your payroll and keeping your accounts; it is in fact precisely because of this that NSF makes grants almost exclusively to institutions rather than to individual scientists, who for the most part haven't the training, the aptitude, the time, or the inclination to take care of such matters. Institutions vary in how much of the other responsibilities of grant management they assume, and how much they leave to the PI, but you have to expect that a certain amount will fall to you. Senior scientists who are PIs of a number of grants, or of very large and complex grants, will usually have an administrative assistant to take on managerial tasks, or they would have no time left to do any science. If you're just getting started, however, this is a luxury you're not likely to have.

Let's take a look at some of the things you may need to deal with in managing your project.

Leading a team. Unless you're the only person working on your project, there are people looking to you for leadership. They expect you to know, and to make clear to them, what they are supposed to do, and to enable them to do it by providing the necessary resources and eliminating interferences. You have to be attuned to their needs as well as your own. You need to develop a clear division of labor, and clear job descriptions based on it for each member of the team – preferably in writing. You need to establish clear, open lines of communication, so they can keep you informed of progress and make sure you know about problems. You need to monitor their work, to be sure they are focused on the task and understand it accurately, while not micromanaging them. If two or more people are working for you, they will have interactions of their own, and you should try to ensure that these are harmonious, and be prepared to arbitrate any disputes that arise. You should provide praise when warranted, correction when necessary, and encouragement regularly. And you should be their advocate and their defender in dealing with the rest of your institution.

Some members of your research team are likely to be students, undergraduate or graduate, and you need to be aware of their special needs. They have many pressures, responsibilities, and deadlines that may conflict with the needs of your project, and you have to accommodate them in ways that allow them to meet those other demands without disrupting or delaying the project.

Also, in working with students you will have to work hard to break the project down into subtasks small enough for them to learn and complete within about three months. This may be harder than just doing the work yourself, but the reward comes in building a team of trained students that can leverage your efforts and enable you to tackle larger projects.

Staying on schedule and within budget. At the beginning of a grant, especially if it's your first one, it may seem as though the time and the money you've been given to do the project are abundant, and you'll have plenty of both for everything you plan to do. This is a dangerous illusion, which may lead you to squander resources in the early stages of the project that you will dearly wish you had back toward the end. In Chapter 2, we mentioned the value of developing a timetable when planning your project. You can make good use of it now, as the basis for a detailed schedule of work. Knowing what you want to accomplish by the end of the grant period, break your project down into a sequence of interim goals and subgoals. Allocate a reasonable, realistic amount of time to each goal and subgoal in the sequence. If the overall total amount of time required adds up to more, or less, than the duration of the grant, go back and rethink and reallocate until you strike a balance. Then translate this timeline into a monthly or weekly calendar, determining what you need to ac-complish during each successive time period – month or week – for the duration of the project. Chances are that seeing the results of this exercise, and realizing how much you have to do in the first months, will motivate you to establish from the beginning of the project the pace you need to maintain throughout it to accomplish your overall goals. A well-thought-out, detailed schedule should serve as a valu-able guide and reference point all through the project. If the course of the project begins to deviate from it significantly, that's a signal that you need either to intensify your efforts or to rethink the project plan and develop a revised schedule.

Besides time, money is the other currency you have to manage carefully. Fortunately, here you'll probably have some help. Your Sponsored Projects Office, or your institution's business office, will be keeping close track of your expenditures under the grant. They have to do this in order to collect grant funds from the funding agency. The office maintaining the grant account will probably give you periodic reports on its status – how much you've spent to date and how much you have left, broken down into the various budget categories. It's in your interest to study these reports carefully, and to make sure that you have an up-to-date awareness of the rate of your spending and how well it conforms to the progress of the project. Clearly, if you run out of grant money before you reach the end of the project, you have a bad problem. Some PIs commit the opposite error, hoarding grant funds rather than spending them systematically on legitimate project costs, and ending up with a surplus of money at the end of the project that they either have to spend quickly and possibly wastefully, or else return to the funding agency. Your responsibility as PI is to avoid both kinds of mistakes, to control the expenditure of your grant so that it best meets the needs of your project throughout its duration. You should think of the budget chronologically, relating it to the work schedule we discussed in the previous paragraph, and determining how much of the budget you should use for each subperiod of the project. As with the time schedule, if a serious deviation from your budget plan arises, you need to attend to it right away, and recast it as necessary to carry out the remainder of your project as effectively as possible.

Extensions and supplements. Basic research is an uncertain enterprise, and no matter how carefully you plan, sometimes things don't work out the way you expected. NSF recognizes this, and has some mechanisms available that offer a measure of flexibility to PIs in managing their projects. One that sees frequent use is called a "no-cost extension." Every grant comes with a specific expiration date, which is the last day that you or your institution can obligate grant funds. As the end of your grant approaches, if you see that you are going to have funds remaining in the grant when it expires, and work remaining in the project to spend them on, you can ask your institution to extend the expiration date of the grant by up to a year, without additional funding (that's the "no-cost" part). NSF has given awardee institutions the authority to do this. The procedure, done through FastLane, is fast and easy. The institution must notify NSF of the extension, and the reasons for it, at least ten days before the expiration date, so you should approach your SPO for the extension well ahead of that time; it's probably best to ask them at least a month before the expiration date.

A second extension requires NSF approval, and is harder to come by, requiring detailed justification based on unusual circumstances. For this reason, it's a good idea to request the full twelve months for your first extension, even if you don't think you'll need it. There's no problem at all for anyone if you use up the rest of the grant funds before the end of the extension.

Extensions remedy the problem of having money left over when the grant expires. What about the opposite situation, when you run out of money before the end of the grant period? Well, it depends on the reason. If you simply didn't manage your budget well, and spent the grant faster than you should have, you have to deal with the consequences. Sometimes, however, something happens that you could not reasonably foresee or prevent – a research assistant unexpectedly quits in the middle of the year, a crucial piece of equipment fails, or a subject becomes ill – and it delays work on your project for some time, while your committed expenses continue to consume your grant, preventing you from completing the project you proposed with the grant you received. If such a misfortune befalls you, you can ask your program officer for supplemental funding. A supplement to your grant is a small amount of extra funding, just enough to patch the hole in your grant that the problem caused, to enable you to complete the project you originally proposed.

You may also want to ask for supplemental funding to do some immediate additional investigation of a surprising new result that has emerged from your work, or to add a bright undergraduate to your research team for the summer. You can't hope to substitute supplemental funding for a renewal proposal, but for small amounts of money, available on short notice, to do something worthwhile in the context of your project, a supplement may be the right mechanism.

It's entirely at the program officer's discretion whether to award a supplement. There is no special pot of money for the purpose, the program officer has to take it from the regular program budget, money that would otherwise be used to fund new projects. However, the program officer has a vested interest in your project, an investment of program resources in the grant you received, and so is eager to see it have every chance to succeed. If you can persuade the program officer of the merits of your case for the supplement, and the amount of extra funding you need is not large, the chances are fairly good that the program officer will provide the help you need. You should approach the program officer informally first, to find out whether a supplement is possible; if the program officer agrees to consider it, your SPO will have to submit a supplemental funding request via FastLane. The request should be submitted at least two months before you need the additional funds.

Supplemental funding can be for up to six months of additional support, and includes an extension of the expiration date, so you'll have the extra time as well as the extra funds to make up for the delay in your project.

Exit the PI. A grant supports a project and a partnership. The partnership is between the institution that receives and administers the grant, and the PI who leads the project. When a funding agency makes a grant, it is on the premise that the PI on the proposal will be the PI on the grant. Part of the evaluation of the proposal is an assessment of the capabilities and track record of the PI; the same proposal from a different PI might not be funded. Therefore, it is a major event when a PI leaves an institution while a grant is active, and the funding agency has to decide how it will deal with the matter.

There are three different possible outcomes, and any one of them might occur, depending on the particular situation. The grant might transfer to the PI's new institution; it might stay at the original institution with a new PI; or the agency might terminate the grant and recover the remaining funds. Termination is the least likely possibility, because the agency wants to see the project it funded continue and succeed. The agency will terminate the grant only if it has no viable alternative – there is some reason why the grant cannot be transferred to another institution, and there is no suitable replacement PI at the original institution.

If you as the PI of an active grant decide to accept an offer to move to another institution, you should begin right away to discuss your grant and what you want to do about it with your current institution. Your interactions with the funding agency will be much easier if you and your current institution speak with one voice in recommending how the agency should act. If you want to take the grant with you, and your present institution agrees, the agency has a regular procedure for transferring the unspent balance of the grant to a different institution. Your program officer will explain to you what you, your present institution, and your new institution all need to do to make this happen.

If you are going someplace where you can't move the grant, perhaps to a corporation or to a foreign institution, and you want to see the project continue in your absence, you can help your current institution identify someone who is suitable to take over your role as PI. This should be someone who is competent to carry on the project as originally proposed, and bring it to a successful conclusion, in the judgment of your program officer. Again, the agency has a procedure for naming a new PI for a funded project.

When you talk to your present institution about transferring your grant, you also need to discuss what to do with the equipment that you have purchased with the grant. The general NSF rule is that the institution receiving the grant owns the equipment, unless the grant specifically states otherwise. If you would like to take the equipment with you to the new institution to use there when you continue the project, your current institution has to agree before you can do so legally.

What if you're not going away permanently, but will be away from your institution for a year or half a year? NSF regards any PI absence of more than three months as a substantial change in the effort devoted to the project, one that the program officer has to approve. When a sabbatical leave or other protracted absence from your institution enters your planning, you need to talk with the program officer early on about possible arrangements for managing your project in your absence. There are various possibilities. You may arrange for someone to act as substitute PI, or suspend the grant for the duration of your absence (with a corresponding extension of the scheduled expiration date), or you may even be able to arrange to continue to manage the project from afar, by profuse e-mail and occasional visits home. The program officer is willing to be flexible, but you have to persuade him or her that your plan will be effective.

Being a manager. There are tons of books on techniques of effective management, and you won't find any guidance here as to which ones you should consult. The best advice I can offer is to try to avoid the stupid mistakes that managers often seem to be prone to, and the best way to learn what those are is extensive reading of the *Dilbert* comic strip, by Scott Adams.

You, PI – in Charge

We've talked a lot about your responsibilities as Principal Investigator, but you also have a considerable amount of authority in that role. If it becomes apparent in the course of the project that you need to move money from one budget category to another, that's your call, within certain constraints – you can't make changes that would affect the amount of indirect costs, or increase your own compensation, without your institution's approval, for example. You need to work with your SPO or business office, whoever is maintaining the grant accounts, when you make budget changes, so they can keep their books straight, but how best to fit the budget to the needs of the project is your decision. Likewise, it's your choice who to hire to work on your project as a research assistant, or technician, or clerical worker, although you have to choose among a pool of people who are eligible for consideration under your institution's rules – for example, your institution may require that research assistants be regularly admitted graduate students.

The funding agency will require its approval for certain major changes in the project. NSF lists in the *Grant Proposal Guide* a specific set of changes which either a grants officer or a program officer must authorize before they can occur. These include some we've already discussed, such as a change in PI, or an extended but temporary absence of the PI; some technical items relating to matters such as cost sharing; and changes in the objectives or the scope of a project, from what was stated in the proposal that resulted in the grant. Other funding agencies will provide you comparable information when they award a grant. You should study this material and discuss with your SPO and your program officer any changes in the project you are considering that you believe may require agency approval. Most of the time, however, the changes you will need to make in the project to adapt to changing circumstances are not so fundamental, and it is within your province as PI to make them.

Care and Feeding of Your SPO, Your Program Officer, and Others

It's your project, but not only yours. There are others who helped to make it possible, and who have a continuing stake and interest in it, and it will benefit the project and you for you to keep them in the information loop as the project progresses. Chief among these are the SPO at your institution and your program officer at the funding agency. There may be others in your particular situation, such as colleagues, administrators, key research subjects, or consultants, that you need to consider as well. The funding agency will impose some formal reporting requirements on you, which we'll come to in the next section, but here we're talking about a more informal and more frequent sort of interaction.

Try to cultivate a relationship with your SPO that has you dropping by every so often just to tell them how things are going, mentioning interesting new developments and potential problems, collecting any suggestions and advice they have to offer, and sharing news and gossip about the institution and the funding agency. They will likely have some regular procedures for you related to managing the grant, such as reporting expenditures and submitting receipts, and you should attend to those promptly and assiduously. Let them know about any substantial interactions you have with the program officer or others at the funding agency. If a serious problem should arise in your project or with your grant, a good SPO is a powerful ally to have, and you want to keep them aware of and interested in your project.

Your program officer also appreciates occasional informal exchanges with you about the project, especially when something noteworthy happens. Part of the program officer's job is to remind the agency regularly of the excitement and significance of the science the program supports. You can help by telling her or him about important new developments, maybe even breakthroughs, that happen in your project. The program officer may get interested enough to ask you to write up a paragraph or two about the accomplishment that he or she can use in a "nugget," a brief account of a research success that the agency can communicate to a broad public audience. Likewise, if you have an opportunity to bring your project to favorable public notice, as through a newspaper article or a TV appearance, be sure to let the program officer know about it, and to send a clipping or a videotape of the occasion. You'd be surprised how valuable that sort of thing is for a government agency.

Don't hesitate to talk about your project with your colleagues, senior and junior, your department chair, your dean, and others at your institution. They are all more interested than you may realize in your progress, your results, and the problems you are dealing with, and they can be valuable allies when you need some.

Renewal Proposals

You probably feel that having received your grant, you are through with proposal writing for a while and can concentrate on your research. So you are, but not for so long a while as you may think. If your project goes well, it is likely to open up new questions and new lines of research that you will want to pursue past the period of your current grant. To do so, you will need further support, which means you will need to apply for a renewal of your grant, which in turn means you will have to write a renewal proposal.

Given the lead time it takes the funding agency to review a proposal, you will need to submit the renewal proposal six to twelve months before the expiration date of your current grant. If your grant's duration is two or even three years, that deadline is going to arrive sooner than you imagine when you start your project. About six months into the project is a good time to start thinking about the future directions of your research, based on your accumulating results and developments in your field. Record these thoughts somewhere where you can augment them and refer to them easily. Allow yourself enough time to develop these notes into a renewal proposal that you can submit in a timely way with less stress and less interruption to your ongoing project.

Reporting Requirements

It should come as no surprise that the agency that funds your project wants you to report periodically on its progress. Agencies all have their own particular reporting requirements; here we'll describe the ones the NSF imposes.

Annual report. Toward the end of each year of your grant's life, reckoning the start date as its birthday, the NSF asks you to provide a summary of the year's activities in your project. FastLane has a Reports module for the purpose. Working your way through the series of FastLane screens, you report on the participants in the project; research and education activities, findings, training, and outreach activities during the year; publications, Web sites, and other products resulting from the project; significant accomplishments during the year, and their contributions to your discipline, to science more generally, and to society; and some miscellaneous special matters, such as updated certifications for human subjects protections and animal welfare.

Every PI has to submit an annual report, but for one group of PIs it has special importance. To understand how that is so, we have to make a small digression to differentiate two types of grants that NSF offers. A program officer may choose to fund a project with a "standard grant" or a "continuing grant." A standard grant is a one-shot deal, with all the grant funds awarded at the outset of the project, whatever the duration of the project may be. A continuing grant is paid on the installment plan, in annual increments. From the program officer's point of view, the continuing grant is a mechanism that allows spreading the cost of the project over several budget years; each year's increment comes from that year's program budget. The annual increments for continuing grants are firm commitments against the program's budget; the program has to reserve the funds committed for that purpose each year before making any new grants.

From the PI's point of view, there isn't a lot of difference between the two types of grants, except in the status of the annual report. For a continuing grant, the program officer must receive and approve the annual report before the next year's funding increment is released. The NSF *Grant Proposal Guide* says that the PI should submit the annual report at least three months before the anniversary date of the grant, to allow plenty of time for the program officer to review and approve the report and release the next year's funding before the project exhausts its current budget. For a standard grant, such a long lead time in submitting the annual report isn't as essential.

Financial reports. NSF has stringent requirements for regular reports on the financial status of a grant. Fortunately for the PI, the SPO or the institution's business office files these reports. Usually the PI isn't even aware that it is happening.

Final project report. When your grant finally expires, whether or not you consider your project completed, you must file a final project report. This report, also filed through FastLane, is much like the annual reports, except that it covers the entire period of the grant. You have 90 days after the expiration date to file the report. If you miss the deadline, you will start receiving regular and increasingly insistent reminders, from NSF and from your institution. Also, you will not be eligible to receive any further grants from NSF, as a PI or a Co-PI, until NSF has received and approved the final project report.

If the grant expiration date is extended, as we discussed earlier in the chapter, the final project report deadline extends along with it. However, wanting to extend the report deadline is not a valid reason for extending the expiration date; that you do only if there are going to be unexpended funds remaining in the grant at the originally scheduled expiration date, and work remaining in the project that requires those funds. Don't think of the final project report as a large or onerous task, because it isn't; you will probably be able to prepare a perfectly adequate one in a day. It is not a comprehensive technical report to your scientific community on the outcome of your project; that you will be doing through the regular channels of scientific publication and dissemination, and there is no time limit on that.

Technical reports. One of your major responsibilities as a PI is to report the results of your research to the scientific community. This is how your project finally contributes to the store of scientific knowledge, which was the purpose of funding it in the first place. You do this through publishing journal articles and monographs, through Web sites, through distributing computer programs you have developed, through doctoral dissertations you supervise, and so on. As these become available, send your program officer a reprint, a copy, a URL, an abstract, or whatever is appropriate (when in doubt as to what is appropriate, ask the program officer). These constitute tangible evidence of your productivity, which is always useful, and they provide the program officer with evidence to demonstrate the excellence of the science the program supports, which helps ensure that the program will continue to have the resources to support you and your fellow scientists in your future projects.

Finis

That's it. We've gone from first idea to final report. Thanks for coming along, and I hope you'll find the advice here helpful. In closing, let me extend to you the same benison that I always offered my PIs at NSF – my best wishes for a successful project!

Appendix A

Glossary of Acronyms

ABR   Accomplishment-Based Renewal
AFOSR   Air Force Office of Scientific Research
ARI   Army Research Institute
ARL   Army Research Laboratory
ARO   Army Research Office
BAA   Broad Agency Announcement
CFDA   Catalog of Federal Domestic Assistance
CISE   Computer and Information Science and Engineering
CR   The Common Rule
CSR   Center for Scientific Review
DARPA   Defense Advanced Research Projects Agency
DEB   Division of Environmental Biology
DGA   Division of Grants and Agreements
DLI   Digital Libraries Initiative
DOD   Department of Defense
EPA   Environmental Protection Agency
EPSCoR Experimental Program to Stimulate Competitive Research
ERE   Environmental Research and Education
GPG   *Grant Proposal Guide*
HHS   (U.S. Department of) Health and Human Services
IACUC   Institutional Animal Care and Use Committee
IGERT   Integrative Graduate Education and Research Traineeship
IRB   Institutional Review Board

IRG	Integrated Review Group
IRS	Internal Revenue Service
ITR	Information Technology Research
MCAA	Minority Career Advancement Award
MRI	Major Research Instrumentation
MRPG	Minority Research Planning Grant
NAS	National Academy of Sciences
NASA	National Aeronautics and Space Administration
NIAID	National Institute of Allergy and Infectious Diseases
NIH	National Institutes of Health
NNI	National Nanotechnology Initiative
NSF	National Science Foundation
OIG	Office of the Inspector General
ONR	Office of Naval Research
ORI	Office of Research Integrity
PA	Program Announcement
PECASE	Presidential Early Career Awards for Scientists and Engineers
PERT	Program Evaluation and Review Technique
PI	Principal Investigator
PPU	Proposal Processing Unit
RFA	Request for Applications
RUI	Research at Undergraduate Institutions
R&D	Research and Development
SGER	Small Grants for Exploratory Research
SPO	Sponsored Projects Office
SRA	Scientific Review Administrator
SRG	Scientific Review Group
STC	Science and Technology Center
TPOC	Technical Point of Contact
URL	Universal Resource Locator

Appendix B

Useful URLs

This is a list of Universal Resource Locators (URLs) that should be useful to the readers of this book. These are the addresses on the Internet and the World Wide Web for funding agencies and other valuable sources of information. The list is current as of September 2003, but you should be aware that these addresses can – and frequently do – change. If an address does not lead you to the place you expected, first check to be sure that you have spelled it correctly – a single letter changed can make the address inoperative. If there are no errors, use a search engine like Google to find the Web site you're looking for.

www.nsf.gov
The home page for the National Science Foundation.

www.nih.gov/icd/
A list of Institutes, Centers, and Offices at the National Institutes of Health, with links to each of the organizations listed.

www.csr.nih.gov/welcome/orgdtls.asp#DRR
A list of the Integrated Review Groups and Scientific Review Groups at the NIH, with names and contact information for professional staff.

www.csr.nih.gov/Committees/rosterindex.asp
The lead page for the rosters of Study Section (panel) members for NIH.

www.csr.nih.gov/Committees/nihlist.htm
Links to the rosters of members of the Advisory Committees for each of the NIH Institutes.

www.niaid.nih.gov/ncn/grants/default.htm
Online tutorials for planning and writing NIH grant proposals and for managing NIH-funded projects.

http://grants1.nih.gov/grants/grant_tips.htm
Grant-writing tip sheets prepared by various NIH staff.

www.afosr.af.mil
The home page for the Air Force Office of Scientific Research.

www.arl.army.mil/aro
The home page for the Army Research Office.

www.ari.army.mil
The home page for the Army Research Institute.

www.onr.navy.mil
The home page for the Office of Naval Research.

www.onr.navy.mil/sci_tech/personnel/proposal1.htm
Instructions for preparing proposals to the Office of Naval Research.

http://www.onr.navy.mil/sci_tech/information/docs/webproprite.pdf
An article written by an Office of Naval Research program officer giving candid and helpful advice about writing research proposals.

www.darpa.mil
The home page for the Defense Advanced Research Projects Agency.

www.darpa.mil/body/overtheyears.html
A brief history of the Defense Advanced Research Projects Agency.

www.cfda.gov
The home page for the Catalog of Federal Domestic Assistance.

www.foundations.org
An online directory of private foundations.

http://fdncenter.org
The home page for The Foundation Center.

Index

ABR. *See* accomplishment-based renewal
abstract, proposal. *See* project summary
accomplishment-based renewal (ABR),
85–6
ad hoc reviewers, 61, 62, 64–7, 70, 75, 76,
79, 82, 95, 96, 112–13, 114, 116, 126–8,
133, 134. *See also* suggesting
reviewers
administrator, project, 22
ADVANCE, 45–6
Advisory Council, NIH, 31, 32, 76
advisory panel, NSF, 61, 62, 67–9, 70, 75,
76, 82, 96, 114–16, 118
AFOSR. *See* Air Force Office of Scientific
Research
Agriculture, U.S. Department of, 103
Air Force Office of Scientific Research
(AFOSR), 35
analysis methods (in a proposal), 66
Animal Welfare Act, 102, 103
animals, research on, 86, 102–3, 125,
144
annual report, 144–5
ARI. *See* Army Research Institute
Army Research Institute (ARI), 36
Army Research Office (ARO), 35
ARO. *See* Army Research Office
ARPA. *See* Defense Advanced Research
Projects Agency
assignment of proposals to programs
(NSF), 81, 83, 111

BAA. *See* Broad Agency Announcement
bibliography. *See* references
biographical sketch (in a proposal), 64,
87–8
breadth (of research topic), 5–6
Broad Agency Announcement (BAA),
35, 36, 37, 38
broader impacts (of a research project),
64, 67, 69, 70, 94, 95, 115
budget, proposal, 19–20, 83, 88–92, 117,
141
budget, revised, 117

Career Development Awards, NIH, 58
CAREER grants, NSF, 11, 44–5, 49, 72,
80
Catalog of Federal Domestic Assistance
(CFDA), 39–40
Center for Scientific Review, NIH (CSR),
30
CFDA. *See* Catalog of Federal Domestic
Assistance
challenge (of research topic), 7–8
collaborators, 88, 89, 99
Common Rule, 99–101
conceptual foundations (section of
proposal), 63, 68
conference grants and proposals, 53–6,
80, 89
continuing grant, NSF, 145
coordination (of large projects), 21